379X4

THE HERITAGE HOUSE
2764 SOUTH ST.
LINCOLN, NE. 68502

FRENCH CAMEO GLASS

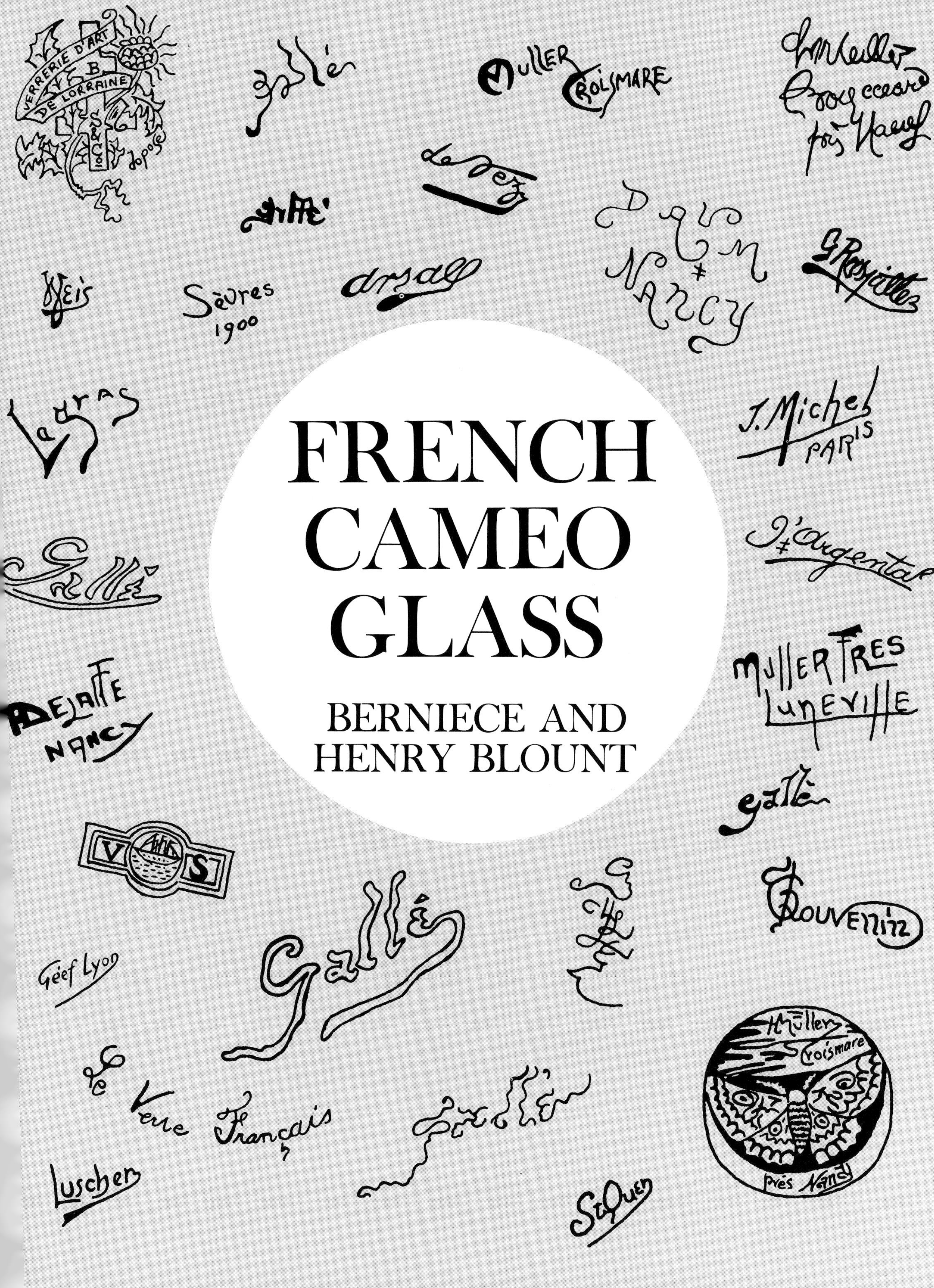

FRENCH CAMEO GLASS

BERNIECE AND HENRY BLOUNT

Library of Congress Catalog Card Number 73-221
ISBN 0-87069-030-2
Copyright © 1968 by Berniece and Henry Blount

Published in the United States of America by
Wallace-Homestead Book Company
Des Moines, Iowa 50305
3rd Printing 1977

Dedicated to:
    Lucy, Henry III, and Amy, and their grandmother,
Elizabeth Rankin Blount.

CONTENTS

Preface 7
History of Cameo Glass 9
Production of Cameo Glass 11
Techniques Other Than Cameo 14
Signatures 15
French Cameo Glass
    Rousseau and Léveillé 16
    Galleé 16
    Daum 20
    Muller 21
    deVez, Mont Joye, and Pantin 22
    Delatte 23
    Le Verre Francais 23
    D'Argental, Richard, and Arsall 24
    Baccarat, Val Saint Lambert, and Saint Louis ...24
    D. Christian Meisenthal, Vallerysthal,
        and Burgun and Schverer 24
    Schneider 25
    Kosta, Reijmyre, and Hadelands 25
    Others 25
Color Illustrations
    Gallé 28
    Daum 66
    Muller 92
    Others 102
    Lamps and Chandeliers 130
    Chinese or Peking 136
    English 137
    American 138
Signatures Copied From Cameo Glass 139
Bibliography 154
Index 156

Preface

Only a small amount of information on French cameo glass is available in libraries in the United States. In this book, available information has been collected, and a number of pieces are illustrated. A more thorough study of this subject is needed.

Our collection of French cameo glass began in June 1962 with the purchase of the scenic D'Argental illustrated in photograph 186 (vase "A"). At that time we were collecting a variety of art and antique items. The beauty and variety found in French cameo glass, and the skilled workmanship evident in this glass stimulated us to concentrate our collecting in this field. All French cameo glass in our collection has been purchased in this country.

Helpful contributions in producing this book have been made by a number of persons, some of whom are: Mrs. Lillian Nassau, who assisted in locating information on the subject; Monsieur Michel Daum, who has been most gracious in providing information about the glass of Daum; Miss Romalyn Heintz, who copied the signatures from the glass; Mr. Jack Koch, who identified foliage in the cameo designs; Mr. Jay Sawtell, who provided translations; Mr. Everett Craft, who reviewed the copy and made many suggestions; Mr. John Graves, who provided corrected information on Schneider glass; Mr. and Mrs. Elliot A. Wysor, who provided information on Burgun, Schverer & Cie.; Mr. Larry Day, who provided advice and help in getting a photographic studio prepared; Mr. Oscar Sparland, who had responsibility for the art work and layout of the book; and Mr. Robert Lyon, who worked hard to assure a good job of printing and binding. We are grateful to those who have generously permitted us to photograph glass in their collections: Mr. and Mrs. William Arbeiter, Mr. and Mrs. Rex Cook, Mrs. Frances Craig, Mrs. Dorothy Galley, Mr. Ray Keller, Mrs. Jeanette Weir, Mr. and Mrs. Don Williams, Mr. and Mrs. Larry Wood, and those who prefer to remain anonymous.

Mr. William Arbeiter deserves special mention. He has been helpful in a number of ways, but particularly with the encouragement and stimulus given to us in this project.

It is our hope that this book will be useful and stimulating to those who have an interest in French cameo glass.

Berniece and Henry Blount.

History of Cameo Glass

Glass has been a medium for artistic expression for many centuries. Known to man for at least 5500 years, it has served him in a great variety of ways as both utilitarian and decorative items. Cameo glass is among the finest and most skilled products of the glassmaking craft.

In the broad definition cameo glass can be defined as any glass in which the surface is cut away to leave a design in relief. This can be in clear or colored glass of a single layer, or in glass with multiple layers of clear or colored glass. The cutting away of the unwanted portion of glass can be accomplished by the use of hand cutting tools similar to those used by sculptors in other media, wheel cutting, and hydrofluoric acid. Most cameo glass pieces with evidence for hand sculpturing and made since the late 1800's have had a large portion of the unwanted glass removed by hydrofluoric acid and have been finished using wheel cutting and hand sculpturing. The major portion of cameo glass produced in the last century has been made utilizing hydrofluoric acid for cutting away most of the unwanted glass and then finishing with mechanical cutting and polishing techniques.

Cameo glass has been made over a span of a number of centuries. Excellent cameo glass was made by Roman craftsmen in the first century B. C. and for a hundred or more years A. D. Good quality wheel engraving of glass surfaces was performed in Europe in the seventeenth and eighteenth centuries; however, with but few exceptions, this was intaglio, although a few examples of cameo relief in clear glass from this period do exist. In about the early eighteenth century the Chinese made opaque glass with carved designs in relief. The mid 1800's saw the beginning of cameo glass work in England. It was not until the latter half of the nineteenth century that French cameo glass was first made and this in very small quantity until after about 1889. In the late nineteenth century and thereafter small amounts of cameo glass were made in the English and French styles in other parts of Europe and in the United States.

Chinese or Peking cameo glass is known to have been made since the eighteenth century. This glass may be of one or more layers and usually has floral designs, occasionally with birds, fish, or other animals carved into the surface. There are some variations in style, but these pieces form a distinct type of cameo glass. Some of the European cameo work shows a very strong oriental influence as do other forms of art in the western world. Peking cameo does not have clear glass between the opaque layers as is frequently the case in cameo glass of English and French styles. Peking cameo was produced by wheel cutting and hand sculpturing.

German, Dutch, Bohemian, and other engravers of glass have produced cameo relief work as early as the seventeenth century. This glass which has some cameo work also generally has intaglio work as well. Fine pieces in this category are known to have been made by F. Zach in Germany in the 1850's and by Karl Pfohl in Bohemia in the 1860's.

Beginning about 1860 cameo glass of the finest quality was made in England. English cameo pieces made before 1880 were carved mostly with hand sculpturing tools with a minimum use of the engraving wheel. After 1880 the engraving wheel almost completely replaced the hand tools in the production of cameo glass in England, although some workers continued to use the hand tools. Hydrofluoric acid was also used to remove unwanted glass in some of the English cameo productions, either as a major technique or in combination with the engraving wheel.

The most outstanding pieces of English cameo glass were produced by the difficult, meticulous, delicate, and skilled hand sculpturing techniques. John Northwood was the earliest of the outstanding English cameo workers, completing his first cameo vase in 1860, and his second in 1873. Northwood worked during a three year period to produce his copy of the famous Portland or Barberini vase which was made about eighteen to nineteen centuries earlier and which is now in the British Museum. Northwood's last and perhaps finest cameo piece is the Pegasus vase which was started in 1876 and completed in 1882, and which now is in the Smithsonian Institution in Washington, D. C. Northwood produced only a few cameo pieces, but he taught the techniques to some very able craftsmen including George Woodall, Thomas Woodall, Frederic Carder, Joshua Hodgett, and others who became internationally known in this field. George Woodall has been credited as being one of the finest carvers ever to work in glass.

The meticulously cut English cameo glass was quite expensive. As cheaper productions utilizing acid-cutting techniques became available, and with the appearance of imitations of cameo glass on the market in the 1890's, the demand for this costly English carved glass declined rapidly.

French cameo glass was probably first produced in about the mid 1880's and reached its peak of popularity between about 1895 and 1905. Thereafter, there was a continued but declining interest in this type of glass, and production ceased in about the mid 1930's. No company produced cameo glass as its only type of art glass and with most it constituted only a minor part of their work.

A number of the major glass companies throughout Europe and the United States produced small amounts of cameo glass, perhaps just to prove that they could produce glass of this type. Because of the skill and cost involved and the lack of greater commercial demand, rather minimal amounts were made. Kosta in Sweden, Loetz in Austria, Reijmyre in Sweden, Hadelands in Norway, Steuben in the United States, Tiffany in the United States, and a number of other companies outside England and France made limited amounts of cameo glass. Frederick Carder of Steuben made a few pieces of hand sculptured cameo of good quality; however, under his direction there was a much larger volume of acid cut-back (ACB) cameo pieces made at Steuben. The combined production of cameo glass by all these companies does not rival the volume of the few major producers of cameo glass in Europe.

Production of Cameo Glass

Several different skills are needed to produce cameo glass. The glass blower produces the blank consisting of one or more layers of glass which is to be subsequently carved. The artist or designer produces a design which is transferred to the surface to guide the cutting of the glass. The engraver then cuts away the unwanted portion of the glass in the surface of the piece to produce the design in relief. The piece may then be finished by polishing and/or decorating with enameling or gilding as desired.

The entire process is planned from start to finish and proceeds in an orderly pattern from the selection of the glass to be used in forming the blank, fo the final finishing processes. The glass blower's task may be relatively easy for one skilled in this work if a rather simply formed vase of single color is to be made. On the other hand, if a vase of relatively complex shape with multiple layers of different colored glass is to be formed as the blank for cameo cutting, then the utmost skill in glass blowing may be required to produce a piece which is satisfactory. Glass selected for each layer must have approximately the same coefficient of expansion as the other layers in the blank. If the glass blower does not select the proper glass for each layer, the piece may crack with heating and cooling, or stresses in the glass may cause it to crack during the cutting process.

To produce designs in relief in glass, the unwanted glass may be removed utilizing hand cutting tools, the engraving wheel, or hydrofluoric acid. Hand sculpturing in the surface of glass using small cutting tools is a delicate, exacting, and slow process requiring considerable skill. The engraving wheel can be used to cut away glass more rapidly than the hand tools and has been used extensively in cameo glass production either as the major method or in combination with hand sculpturing or acid cutting techniques.

Hydrofluoric acid erodes glass, and therefore this acid can be used to dissolve or cut away portions of glass exposed to it. Various kinds of wax are resistant to the action of hydrofluoric acid. Cameo relief designs in glass can then be produced by covering portions of glass with wax, and then dipping the glass into hydrofluoric acid, permitting the unprotected areas of glass to be cut away by the acid. The process has been referred to as the acid cut-back (ACB) technique. The depth of the acid cutting can be controlled by the strength of the acid and the duration of the exposure of the glass to the acid. Some cameo pieces are made with a single acid cutting, whereas others may have several acid cuttings requiring a different wax pattern on the glass surface for each acid bath. Some intricate and complex designs can be produced by this acid cutting process.

For one to produce the planned final result in the cameo piece, layers of required colors of glass must be formed in the proper order and proper thickness in the blank prepared for the engraver. The design must be appropriate for the size and shape of the glass blank which has been produced by the glass blower. The engraver using hand sculpturing, the engraving wheel, or acid cutting, or combinations of these techniques, must cut away the surface of the glass to the varying depths to expose the proper color and design according to the predetermined plan. Sometimes the designer and engraver may alter the predetermined plan to take advantage of some fault in the glass blank with which they have to work. For example, an unwanted streak of color or a bubble may be incorporated into the design to appear as though planned. If acid cutting is used, the engraver will usually use wheel cutting to finish the cutting process, and he may then polish the surface of the glass. Occasionally, pieces have further work in the form of decorative enameling, painting, or gilt. Now and then the pieces may have tops or bases of silver or other metals.

There is a considerable variety in cameo glass. Some varieties are relatively easily produced by cutting back portions of the surface with acid techniques and the relief outlines frequently decorated with painting or enameling or with gold gilt. As the number of layers of glass increases and as the engraving wheel is used more in the cutting process, the pieces become more complex and more difficult to produce. The greatest skill and time are required to produce pieces by sculpturing with hand tools.

There are a number of techniques in glass which may be found in association with cameo relief work, including: intaglio, padding, cabochon application, marquetry, and pâte de verre.

Intaglio is the process of engraving or carving by making cuts in the surface. Intaglio designs are produced by impressions cut into the surface. This is the opposite of cameo in which designs are left in relief after cutting away surrounding glass. Examples of cameo pieces which have small amounts of intaglio work are shown in photographs 150, 157, 161, and 224 (vases "B" and "D").

Cabochon is defined as a precious stone which is cut in convex shape and which is polished but not faceted. In glass the term cabochon refers to applied bits of glass which have the appearance of jewels and which may or may not have carving in the surface (see photographs 18 (vase "B"), 108, 123, 143, 145, and 231).

Padding in glass is a technique in which glass is applied to the surface while the blank is still hot. The applied glass may be left as a mass in the surface, worked into a design, or carved. The Schneider vase in photograph 190 is an example in which padding has been used with the applied glass carved into a stylized flower blossom. The pink flowers in photograph 135 were produced in glass applied to the surface by the padding technique with carving in the applied glass. Vases in photographs 89, 98, 125, 136 (vase "A"), and 138 (vase "B") show a variation of the padding technique.

Marquetry is defined as a decoration made in furniture with thin pieces of wood, ivory, metal, etc., in which the pieces are fitted together to form a design. In 1897, Gallé introduced a technique in glass which he called "marqueterie de verre". This is not cameo. The design is produced by pressing semimolten glass into the surface of the blank before cooling. If desired, the glass may then be carved. If a design in relief is produced by the carving, then this carved portion might be considered as cameo. The design in the vase in photograph 6 was made using the marquetry technique.

Pâte de verre (paste of glass) is not cameo but is a type of glass in which powdered glass is molded and then fused by heating. The surface may be cut in the finishing process and designs in relief produced by this cutting might be considered to be cameo. Pâte de verre was produced in antiquity, and the technique was revived in the latter half of the 19th century. In the late 1800's and in the 1900's there were a number of persons who used this technique in at least some of their work, including: Henri Cros, Eugène Rousseau, Emile Gallé, the Daum brothers, Albert Dammouse, George Despret, Francois Décorchemont, G. Argy-Rousseau, and Almeric Walter.

Signatures

The signing of paintings, sculpture, and other types of art has been a common practice for many years; however, the signing of art glass was unusual until after Gallé started regularly signing his works. Since that time many decorators and manufacturers have signed their art glass. A variety of methods has been used to place signatures on cameo glass including: gold gilt, enamel, acid etching, intaglio cutting, and cameo relief. Signature identifications in French cameo glass consist of initials, a name, a company monogram, a design, or a combination of these, and are often associated with the name of a town, a city or sometimes with the name "France." Companies which sold the glass have been known to either add their name, or replace the manufacturer's name with their own. Many manufacturers of French cameo glass worked in the areas of Nancy and Paris, and many in the Nancy area included the cross of Lorraine with the signature.

Unsigned cameo glass in the French style may be difficult to identify as to the manufacturer or the country in which it was made. A dishonest person may be tempted to add a signature to unsigned pieces, as signed glass often sells at a higher price. Lack of a signature does not mean the glass is not good, as some unsigned cameo is of outstanding quality.

Utilizing the signature to establish the date of manufacture of French cameo may, in some cases, be reasonably accurate; however, in general, companies used essentially the same signatures over a period of years. In unusual instances cameo glass was dated when made.

On pages 139 through 153 there are 192 signatures reproduced in actual size from cameo glass. Signatures can be seen in a number of the color photographs.

French Cameo Glass

Rousseau & Léveillé—

Eugène Rousseau showed great skill in working with glass and, among his other works, produced layered glass and did some engraving in glass surfaces in about 1884 and 1885. Rousseau was respected among the professional art glass workers of his day, although he enjoyed only limited commercial success. Rousseau pieces are rare and unless signed, may be difficult to attribute with reasonable certainty to Rousseau. When Rousseau retired in 1887, Léveillé took over his plant and in subsequent years produced a variety of art glass including a small amount of glass with relief carving in the surface.

Gallé—

Emile Gallé was and is the dominant figure in French cameo glass and was perhaps the most outstanding person working in glass in the Art Nouveau period. He was student and teacher, worker and director, craftsman and artist. He demonstrated fine skills as botanist, chemist, author, and businessman in addition to those shown in his work with ceramics, furniture, and glass. A man of considerable energy and drive, he researched his problems well and experimented thoroughly. Gallé was an innovator. He developed a number of new techniques in glass production and decoration, and improved on a number of others. He was one of the few persons to master all the skills required to produce a quality piece of cameo glass from the forming of the blank to the final finishing processes. He was a master in his chosen field. He truly deserved the title "Wizard of Nancy".

Emile Gallé's father, Charles Gallé, had a shop in Nancy and sold glassware from Meisenthal and pottery from Saint-Clément, both of which were largely decorated with his own designs and intended for everyday use. The faience was signed "Gallé" or "GR" for Gallé and Reinemer, his wife's family name, and stenciled with the name "Saint-Clément." Exposure to his father's work undoubtedly stimulated Emile's interest along these lines.

Emile Gallé was born in Nancy, France in 1846. As a young man, Emile Gallé attended schools at Nancy and spent much of his spare time in reading and study. He developed a considerable interest in nature which was a continued inspiration to him. One of his recreations was walks in the Lorraine countryside which afforded opportunity for study of the flora and fauna of the area. Plants and insects native to that area served as subjects for decoration of much of his works in later years.

In 1865 Emile Gallé left Nancy and went to study at the art school in Weimar. He then studied glass-making at Meisenthal and ceramic work at Saint-Clément, where at both places he had the advantage of his father's guidance. In 1870 his studies were interrupted by a period of service in the French army for approximately one year during the Franco-Prussian War.

In 1871 his father was showing at the "Arts of France" exhibition in London, and Emile's trip with his father afforded an opportunity to study at the South Kensington Museum and the Botanical Gardens there. Shortly thereafter he spent some time studying in Paris. In 1873 a large house was built by Emile's father, and a studio and workshop was built by Emile. As early as 1865 Emile made some designs for his father's pottery decoration at Saint-Clément and continued some work for and with his father until Charles Gallé retired in 1874 and turned the business over to Emile. In 1875 Emile married, and he and his wife made their home in a section of his father's large house. Emile's wife inherited a mirror shop which was sold and was never a part of the Gallé glassworks.

Gallé's earlier work in glass was primarily with clear and transparent glass which was decorated with enamel. In the 1880's he made some clear glass which contained colored fragments. He may well have admired and been influenced by the enamel work of Joseph Brocard and the fine quality work in glass of Eugène Rousseau; however, he developed a style which is clearly his own.

Gallé exhibited in Paris in 1878 with his "Clair de Lune" glass of pale blue coloring his best received product. In 1884 he exhibited a variety of decorative glass in Paris. Between 1884 and 1889 was a relatively dormant period for Gallé as far as glass output was concerned. This was apparently a time of study, research, and development.

In 1889 he presented much new work at the Paris exposition, and this was well received and added considerably to his reputation as a maker of fine glass. It was at this 1889 Paris exposition that he introduced his multi-layered glass with surface cutting. His cameo glass was widely acclaimed, and this technique was soon thereafter to be used by other glass manufacturers. Gallé continued to make this type glass throughout the remainder of his life, and it is this type glass for which he is best known. Glass inspired by and having quotations from poetry were named "verriere paralante". Scenic pieces which were first made in the 1890's he referred to as "paysages de verre". Other variations in his glass include the incorporation of metallic foils between layers of glass, application of glass to the surface in the form of cabochons, padding or marquetry, combination of streaks and "clouds" of glass within a layer, and decoration with enamels and gold gilt.

The carved glass of Gallé has been classified into three groups: (1) the unique, one-of-a-kind pieces; (2) pieces of good quality, well carved and made in limited quantity; and (3) the large quantity of the commercial production in which similar designs were repeatedly used with variation in shapes, sizes, and colors of the cameo pieces. Because of the complexity of manufacturer, variations in glass coloring, and perhaps some attempt to avoid duplications, it is most unusual to find identical pieces of cameo produced by Gallé.

Some engravers in the seventeenth and eighteenth centuries initialed some of their finest works, and a few glass firms put marks on their wares. Gallé, however, was the first to put his name on every piece made by him or produced at his factory. Gallé apparently enjoyed having his name signed, and he signed the glass in a variety of ways. (See signatures pages 139-144). Before Gallé popularized the signing of glass, it was a rarity to find signatures in glass. After Gallé's success, many glassmakers started signing their products.

During the late 1890's there was increasing demand for Gallé's glass, and in 1900 he had about three hundred employees with outlets for his glass in Nancy, Paris, and several major cities in Europe.

At the 1900 International Exhibition in Paris, Gallé had an outstanding exhibit with many fine pieces of glass and with a working glass furnace in the center of the display. He was highly acclaimed, and this experience was probably the high point of his career.

Gallé was honored as the head of the Ecole de Nancy (School of Nancy). Membership in this "school" consisted of a number of men who had achieved prominence in their particular fields, including: Hesteaux, a potter; the Daum brothers, manufacturers of fine glass; Victor Prouvé, a painter and artist in other media; Majorelle, the outstanding furniture maker; and others.

Gallé continued to produce some glass of masterpiece quality into the final year of his life. In September 1904 at the age of 58, Emile Gallé died.

The Gallé glassworks continued in operation at Nancy until 1914 with Emile Lang as manager and Victor Prouvé, Gallé's longtime friend, as family advisor. Production was interrupted during World War I but was resumed at Epinay after the War, where there was continued production until 1935.

After 1904, the factory lacked the inventive genius of Gallé and products were those utilizing established techniques, mostly acid cut glass on frosted backgrounds. Between 1904 and 1914 the signature of Gallé was often preceeded by a star. During this time, however, there were pieces known to bear the name Gallé without the star. The star in the signature was apparently not used in the production after 1914.

The quality of the glass produced by the Gallé factory after his death gradually deteriorated, and by the time the factory closed, the reputation of Gallé glass suffered considerably. Had production stopped at the Gallé factory with Emile Gallé's death, or had the name Gallé been dropped from the product at that time, the reputation of Emile Gallé would undoubtedly not have suffered so greatly.

This dedicated and talented man has left to those who followed an increased knowledge in the use of glass as an art form.

Daum.

Daum has been an important name in glass production in France since the late 1800's. In 1875 Jean Daum, father of Auguste (1853-1909) and Antonin (1864-1930), acquired a glass factory in Nancy and gave it the name "Verrerie de Nancy". In their early years glass tableware, which was usually decorated, was the major commercial item manufactured by the Daums. In 1887 Auguste and Antonin assumed direction of the glass factory.

The Daums, like Gallé, were also undoubtedly influenced by the enamel work of Joseph Brocard and the glass work of Eugène Rousseau, and were strongly influenced by the work of Gallé. The Daums, who also exhibited in Paris in 1889, were so inspired with Gallé's work and his success at this exhibition that shortly thereafter they changed their line of work in glass to the production of art glass.

Throughout the 1890's and into the 1900's the Daums produced cameo glass. They made some unique pieces of merit, but most of their creative works served as models for their industrial production. The Daums demonstrated skill in their wheel engraving. It is their acid-cut work with enamel and gold decoration, however, which has come to be recognized as their more typical style, and which accounts for a large portion of their cameo glass production. Daum proved a versatile manufacturer of art glass and produced a variety of styles in cameo glass, including commercial pieces with repetition of design and form as well as singular pieces of outstanding quality.

The Daums utilized many techniques developed by Gallé and others. Nevertheless, they developed some techniques and their own artistic style. They gained the respect of Gallé as reflected in some of his writings and as demonstrated by the fact that they were included as members of the Ecole de Nancy (School of Nancy).

Daum suffered the pressures of the other art glass manufacturers with the passage of time and the change in the types of glass which the public demanded. Daum adapted to these changes by producing different types and styles in glass.

Auguste Daum died in 1909, with Antonin continuing as head of the factory. About 1920 Paul Daum became director. At this time the glass produced was much more simple in form, and many of the complex techniques of earlier years were not used. Since 1945 Henri and Michel Daum have continued to produce decorative clear crystal in a modern style. Michel Daum is presently the artistic director of the Cristallerie de Nancy, and his brother Jacques is commercial director. The Daum glassworks is presently producing freely-blown crystal of high quality.

Daum signatures are found in gold gilt, acid etched, engraved with acid or wheel cutting, enameled, or in cameo relief. The signature almost always appears with the name "Nancy" and with the cross of Lorraine. Now and then the name "France" appears without the name "Nancy." Modern pieces are stamped and etched with the names "Daum" and "France," and the cross of Lorraine.

Muller.

The Muller brothers worked for Gallé before they established their glassworks. Most of the glass produced at Luneville was signed "Muller Fres Luneville," although it was sometimes signed "Muller Frēres Luneville," "Muller," or "Luneville." At Croismare, glass was signed in the following ways: "Muller Croismare"; "Muller"; Croismare"; "Muller Croismare Nancy"; or "Croismare Nancy." The explanation for the occasional appearance of the name "Nancy" is uncertain.

The Luneville cameo glass was produced almost entirely by acid cutting. A greater variety of styles is evident in the Croismare cameo pieces with both acid and wheel cutting used. In some of the Croismare pieces wheel engraving was the major cutting technique. Photographs on pages 92 through 101 demonstrate a reasonable cross-section of the cameo glass of the Muller brothers and illustrate some of the fine quality in their work. The exact dates of operation of the Luneville and Croismare glassworks by the Muller brothers are unknown to us, although the most active period of production has been stated to be from about 1905 into the early 1930's.

deVez, Mont Joye, and Pantin

Cameo glass bearing the names "deVez," "Mont Joye," and "Pantin" was produced by the same company. This company was founded by E. S. Monot at LaVillette near Paris in 1850. In 1859, known as "Cristallerie de LaVillette" the company was transferred to Pantin, at that time a suburb of Paris and now a part of Paris. After F. Stumpf joined the company in 1868 it became "Monot & Stumpf." In 1873 Monot's son joined the company and the name changed to "Monot, Pere et Fils et Stumpf." About 1894 the company became known as the "Stumpf, Touvier, Violette & Company." About 1900 the glass works became known as "Cristallerie de Pantin" and was operated by Saint-Hilaire, Touvier, de Varreux & Company".

Monsieur de Varreux was the firm's art director and signed many pieces of cameo with the alias "deVez". An elaborate monogram of the company's initials was used to sign some pieces of Pantin glass. Pieces signed "Mont Joye" were generally acid cut and decorated pieces. The styles of pieces signed "deVez," "Mont Joye," and "Pantin" tend to be different, although there is occasionally some similarity. Note the deVez vase "A" in photograph 174 has some of the features of the Pantin vases in photograph 207.

Legras.

August J. F. Legras started work in glass in 1864 at Saint-Denis near Paris, and continued production until about 1914. He produced a variety of art glass, much of which can be classified as cameo glass. Some of his glass is of good quality with multi-layered and well-cut glass; but, much of his work presently available is of simple acid cutting with decorative work which occasionally leaves much to be desired.

Legras developed styles which were his own and gained the respect of other glass workers of his time. That he produced some fine glass with originality is evidenced by his being awarded the Grand Prix at the Universal Exhibition in Paris in 1900.

Delatte.

Andre Delatte started glass production in Nancy in 1921. His cameo glass is almost entirely layered and acid cut, and sometimes has evidence for some wheel cutting. His glass is signed "ADelatte Nancy." His style of work is similar to that of a number of his predecessors.

Le Verre Francais

Le Verre Francais cameo glass was produced in Paris and has a rather distinct style. Usually of only two layers and with a single acid cutting, both the thinner outside and thicker inside layers are almost always mottled, streaked or clouded with glass of varying colors. Both layers generally change in color from top to bottom. Floral designs were chosen as the decorative motifs. Reference to photographs numbered 180, 181, 182, 240 (vase "A") and 242 (vase "C") can serve better than words to demonstrate such a style in cameo glass. Others made cameo glass of this general type, including the Daum brothers. The signature is usually with the name "Le Verre Francais" etched or engraved at the top of the base, with the name "Charder" occasionally appearing in cameo relief somewhere in the lower portion of the body of the piece. A small bit of striped or "candy cane" glass was sometimes imbedded into the base of the cameo piece as the identifying mark of the company. In some instances both the engraved or etched signature and the "candy cane" mark appear in the same piece.

D'Argental, Richard and Arsall

Among the other more frequently encountered names in French cameo glass available in the market today are: D'Argental, Richard, and Arsall. All pieces encountered by the authors with these names are multilayered, acid-cut cameo with either floral or scenic designs. D'Argental apparently had a preference for dark pieces, particularly those with caramel-colored backgrounds and outside layer of dark reddish-brown glass. Richard and Arsall generally used much brighter colors. Richard demonstrated a greater degree of variety in both colors and shapes than either D'Argental or Arsall.

Baccarat, Saint Louis, and Val Saint Lambert

Baccarat and Saint Louis of France and Val Saint Lambert of Belgium are all large glass companies and each produced a variety of types of glass. All three produced cameo glass, much of which was in a similar style with a thin layer of transparent colored glass on a clear glass base with acid cutting. Designs were usually floral and backgrounds generally had geometric or delicate pattern designs cut in relief in the clear glass. They also produced some cameo in layered semi-opaque glass with floral and scenic designs. Wheel cutting is occasionally evident in the surfaces.

D. Christian Meisenthal, Vallerysthal, and Burgun and Schverer.

Cameo glass signed D. Christian Meisenthal, Vallerysthal, and Burgun and Schverer is infrequently found in the market today, yet glass with these names is generally of unusually good quality. Skill in glass blowing, designing, and carving is usually evident in these pieces. Surface wheel cutting was often used. Decorating, when present, is usually very well done. Burgun and Schverer pieces are signed with a rather complex monogram containing a thistle, the cross of Lorraine, and within a ribbon the following: "VERRERIE D'ART DE LORRAINE" and "B S & Co." D. Christian Meisenthal and Vallerysthal pieces are signed with the names etched, engraved, or in cameo relief. Cameo pieces made by Christian Meisenthal and by Burgun and Schverer were produced at Meisenthal.

Schneider.

The Schneider glassworks was founded in 1903 at Epinay-sur-Seine by two brothers, Charles and Ernest Schneider. Ernest was manager and administrator. Charles was art director and supervisor of the art glass department. The Schneider plant moved to Lorris, France, in 1962 and is still in operation there.

Charles Schneider was born at Chateau-Thierry in 1881 and moved to Nancy as a small child where he grew up. Charles studied under Emile Gallé, worked in the Gallé factory for a time, and also worked as a designer for the Daum brothers. The art glass of Schneider either was made by him or was closely supervised by him in the different stages of production. Art glass was produced between 1903 and 1930; crystal wares and lightly colored glass were made until 1945; and only clear crystal has been produced since 1945. Cameo glass was a relatively minor part of the art glass production of Schneider, with both acid and wheel cutting techniques used. Pieces are signed "Schneider" with or without an outline of a vase by the signature, and with or without the name "France" by the signature.

Kosta, Reijmyre, and Hadelands.

The Kosta glassworks in Sweden began cameo glass production in 1897 with Gunnar Gunnarson Wennerberg as designer. In 1901 Wennerberg left Kosta and the company ceased cameo glass production. A. E. Bowman had assisted Wennerberg at Kosta. When cameo production stopped at Kosta, Bowman moved to the glass factory at Reijmyre where he produced cameo glass designed by Ferdinand Boberg. In 1911 Bowman moved to the Hadelands Glassverk in Norway where he produced in that year over one hundred signed cameo pieces. The cameo glass at Kosta, Reijmyre, and Hadelands was in the style of standard or commercial Gallé.

Others

Maurice Marinot entered the glass trade in 1911. His first work was with enamelware and later in glass with deep geometric engraving. He is best known for his work in cased, colored glass with colorful effects produced by chemical staining. Some cameo glass was made by Marinot; however, he is not well known for this technique. He was very skilled in glass work and developed an international reputation in this field. Marinot was, for a time, head of the Ecole de Nancy (School of Nancy), a position previously held by Emile Gallé.

Edward Michel was an engraver of glass who worked for Rousseau and Léveillé. He later made a small amount of good quality cameo glass under his own name. The pieces in this book which are signed Michel (photographs 202 (vase "A"), 202 (vase "B"), and 213 (vase "A"); signatures #140 and #145) are not the work of Edward Michel, but another Michel.

Loetz (photograph 209 and 219 ("A") and Moser (vase "A" in photograph 217) of Austria are well known in the art glass field but produced only small amounts of cameo glass.

Paul Nicolas worked for Gallé and later produced cameo glass. Jacques Gruber worked for Daum and later became famous as a maker of stained glass windows. The cameo plaque in photograph 212 is signed by Gruber.

In addition to producers previously mentioned, many other manufacturers of art glass during the 1890's and early 1900's made cameo glass in the French style in limited quantities. On the following pages some examples are included in the photographs with signature reproductions.

Photographs of
and
Signatures from
FRENCH CAMEO GLASS

Many French cameo glass pieces are illustrated which demonstrate a variety of types and styles by a number of companies and artists.

Signatures are copied in actual size from these cameo pieces.

This photograph is included to give a better appreciation of the relative sizes. Each of these pieces is presented in subsequent pictures.

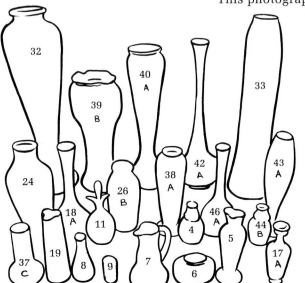

Numbers in the accompanying diagram refer to the photograph in which the piece is illustrated.

This photograph is included to give a better appreciation of the relative sizes. Each of these pieces is presented in subsequent pictures.

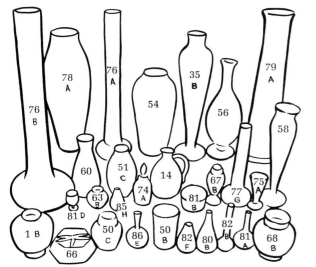

Numbers in the accompanying diagram refer to the photograph in which the piece is illustrated.

29

1.

A. Gallé. 7″ tall. Unfinished vase. The acid cutting has been completed, but the finishing work was not completed. See discussion below.

B. Gallé. 7″ tall. Different in color but almost identical in design to "A". Both acid and hand work are evident in this finished piece. (Signature #50).

After the glass blower formed the blanks for "A" and "B" with two layers of glass, the external surfaces were smooth and uniform in color as in the base portion of "A". The artist then outlined a design on the surface of each vase to guide the cutting. The portions to be spared from the cutting by the acid were coated with a wax which is resistant to the acid. With each succeeding acid bath, either more wax was removed or applied so that the acid cut the appropriate areas to proper depths to produce the desired design.

The acid cutting in "A" has been completed, and it is now ready for the hand work which was not done. "A" has been subjected to two acid baths with three glass thicknesses therefore evident in the surface. In the lower portion of "A" in the photograph, there is a signature which is not considered to be authentic as an incised signature of this type would not be present at this stage and is crude cutting for a Gallé signature.

"B" is a finished Gallé vase in the oriental style with an almost identical cameo pattern to that in "A". Careful inspection of these two pieces illustrates the amount of hand work necessary after the acid cutting.

2.   3.

Gallé. 12" tall. (In the collection of Mr. and Mrs. William Arbeiter).

"2" and "3" are the same vase photographed in the same position with the only difference being in the lighting. In "2" there is front lighting with reflected light from the piece. In "3" the light is predominantly from behind the vase with the camera picking up primarily light transmitted through the vase.

Many French cameo pieces will have a very different appearance when viewed with a light behind as contrasted with light from the front. Some French cameo vases are most beautiful when viewed in a window with sunlight behind them; others may have an interesting appearance only when lighted from the front. Lighting demonstrating its best features is essential to fully appreciate each cameo piece. Photographs in this book all have some illumination from the front, but many have greater or lesser amounts of illumination from behind the cameo pieces.

4.

Gallé. 6½″ tall. This piece demonstrates very skilled work by the glass blower as well as in the cameo work. This vase is beautifully shaped with four layers of glass. The green glass is worked only into the upper portion. There are 13 bands or ribs of colored glass which extend from the center of the base, throughout the body, and into the very top lip of the vase. There is evidence for hand work with the engraving wheel throughout the surface with expertly carved foliage. Considerable skill and experience are necessary in the planning and execution of pieces of this quality. (Signature #17).

5.

Gallé. 13″ tall. Glass for the blossoms was applied while the blank was still hot, and the blossoms were subsequently carved to produce the present appearance. Acid cutting work is evident in the surface of this vase; however, the foliage and much of the background have been subjected to considerable wheel engraving. (Signature #48).

6 Gallé. 4" tall with a roughly ovoid body measuring approximately 6½" by 4½" in greater and lesser dimensions. The colored glass for the lillies and leaves was applied into the surface while the vase was still hot, a technique known as marquetry. The entire external surface of the vase was then enclosed in transparent glass, with cameo relief in the transparent glass over the colored glass lillies and leaves. It is the wheel engraving in the clear glass which constitutes the cameo work in this vase. There is wheel engraving in portions of the surface to give a "hammered metal" appearance. (Signature #26).

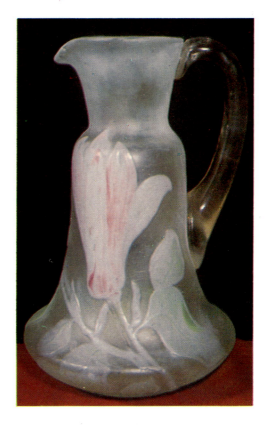

7 Gallé. 9½" tall. The only portion of the external surface which was not subjected to the cutting of the engraving wheel is the handle. The floral design was very skillfully carved. (Signature #24).

33

8

Gallé. 8″ tall. The cobweb outline is produced by acid cutting, however, there is much hand engraving of the leaves trapped in this cobweb. This piece was apparently made for the American or English market as a stamp on the bottom states "Made in France", "Special". (Signature #1).

9 Gallé. 4½″ tall. The stopper has been placed beside the bottle for the photograph. The design in the metal top is not the same as the finely sculptured carnation which is present in the body of this bottle. The signature "E. Gallé" is carved into one of the leaves of the carnation. The metal top, bearing the name of Shreve and Company, has many open areas so that when the stopper is removed and the lid replaced, scented material in the bottle is exposed to the room air. (Signature #58).

10

Gallé. 11⅝″ tall. The red leaves on the frosted clear class have been carved with wheel cutting. Close inspection will also reveal portion of a sculptured leaf in the clear glass in the mid portion of this stick vase. (In private collection). (Signature #65).

11

Gallé. 11″ tall. Three layers of glass with two acid cuttings and some wheel engraving form this decanter. The inside of this decanter has been bathed in acid to produce the frosted appearance. A bubble is incorporated into the upper portion of the stopper and another into the lower portion of the stopper. (Signature #25).

12 Gallé. 4½″ tall. The floral design in the surface is produced by wheel engraving. The signature in cameo relief on the bottom was produced by acid engraving. (In the collection of Mrs. Jeanette Weir). (Signature #55).

13

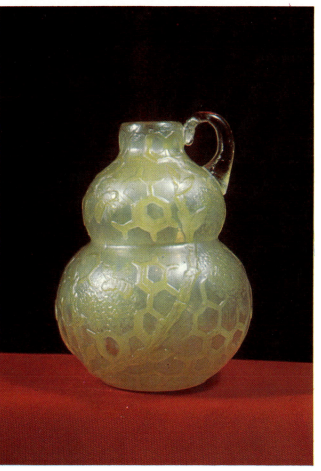

Gallé. 3½″ tall. This small handled bottle has two bees and a honeycomb carved in the surface using acid cutting. In one of the cells of the honeycomb the letters "E. G." with the cross of Lorraine are cut into the surface. The signature on the bottom is in cameo relief and a paper Gallé sticker has also been applied to the bottom of this vase. (In private collection). (Signature #53).

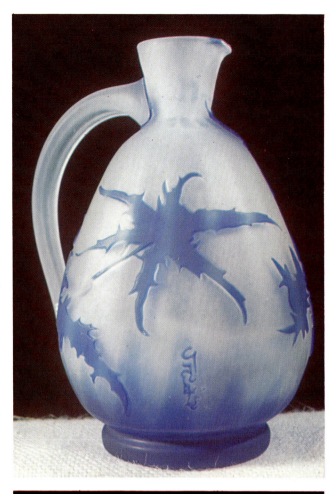

14 Gallé. This Gallé pitcher is 8½" tall. There are two layers of glass with a single acid cutting. Sixteen bands of blue glass radiate from the central portion of the base into the body of this pitcher. Note the number "18" in signature. (See signature #44).

15 Gallé. 8¾" tall. The blossoms and much of the foliage in the design are formed by colored material incorporated between layers of glass. Foliage in cameo relief in the pale green transparent outside layer of glass corresponds with and is over the colored outlines of the underlying colored material in only a few areas. (In the collection of Mrs. Dorothy Galley).

16

(A) Gallé. Bud vase, 13¾" tall. The body and base portions were made separately. Note the many ribs in the body of this vase. There is acid work evident in the surface. In the small white floral portions of the Queen Ann's lace, decoration has been applied with enameling. (In private collection). (Signature #23).

(B) Gallé. This bud vase is 12" tall and has a symmetrical and somewhat stylized decoration. The number "18" appears beneath the Gallé signature. (Signature #15).

17

(A) Gallé. 10½" tall. An orchid is sculptured in the surface of this vase. Silver foil is incorporated between layers of glass. The decorative signature on the base is included in an orchid design. (Signature #69).

(B) Gallé. 9" tall. An orchid is also carved into the surface of this vase. Silver foil is incorporated between layers of glass. (Signature #66).

18

(A) Gallé. 15½" tall. Wheel sculpturing has produced an orchid design in the surface of this vase. Silver foil is incorporated between the layers of glass. This vase is an example in which Gallé mixed chemicals into the glass which when heated produced tiny bubbles. Close inspection reveals hundreds of tiny bubbles within this glass. (Signature #32).

(B) Gallé. 17" tall. The floral design carved in the surface of this vase was produced primarily with acid cutting although there is some wheel engraving throughout much of the surface of this vase. A small amount of metallic foil has been incorporated between the layers of glass. Cabochons have been applied to form the center of the flower in the lower portion and to form the bud for the flower in the upper portion as seen in the photograph. An unusual incised Gallé signature appears in the bottom of this vase. (Signature #59).

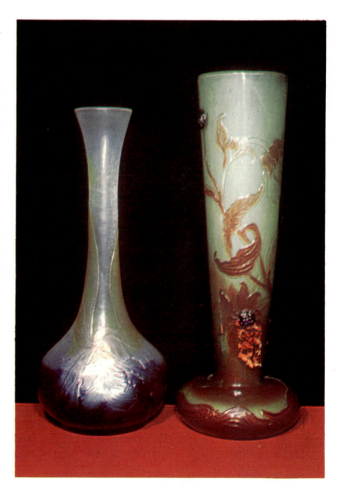

19

Gallé. 12" tall. This ice blue forest winter scene was produced from a two layer glass blank with a single acid cutting. Two birds in flight were then enameled onto the surface. (Signature #30).

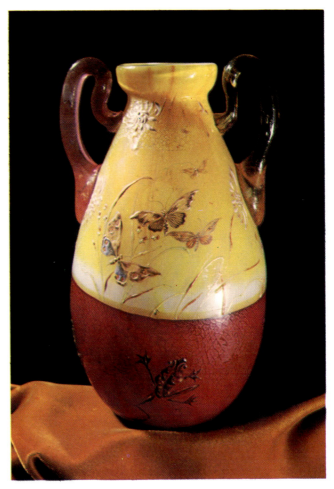

20

Gallé. 11" tall. Enameled flowers, butterflies, and frogs and some gold decoration are present in the surface of this vase. This is not primarily a cameo piece although there are some stylized frogs and flowers outlined in acid cut cameo relief at the base of the vase and some about the handles (Signature #67).

21

Gallé. 7½" tall. The flowers and butterflies are outlined in cameo relief and enameled. There are two layers of glass in this vase which was subjected to a single acid cutting. (In the collection of Mr. and Mrs. William Arbeiter). (Signature #20).

22

Gallé. This leaf-shaped plate is 10½" by 7½" in greater and lesser dimensions. Note the folded edge. The glass is pale amber and has been subjected to a single acid cutting producing cameo outlines with subsequent enamel and gilt decoration.

23

Gallé. This bowl is 4" tall and 8½" in diameter. This amber glass has been subjected to acid cutting which outlines the nasturtiums in relief, and the vase was then decorated with enamel and gold gilt. (Signature #43).

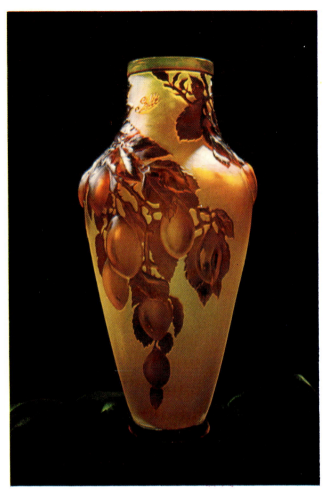

24

Gallé. 15½" tall. This vase was mold blown. The rather prominent projections of the plums and leaves are produced largely by the shape of the mold, although there are two acid cuttings in the surface of this vase.

25

Gallé. 13" tall. Greengage plums decorate this mold blown vase which has had three acid cuttings in the surface.

26

Gallé. Each of these two mold blown vases is 11½" tall with fuchsia decoration with three acid cuttings. ("A" is in the collection of Mr. and Mrs. Don Williams).

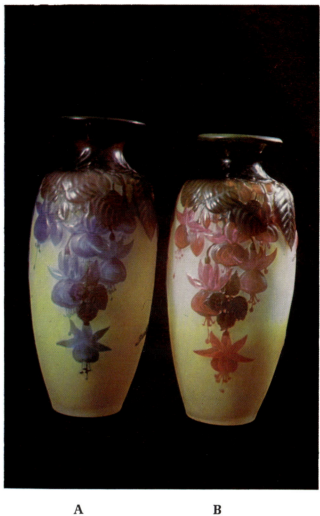

A   B

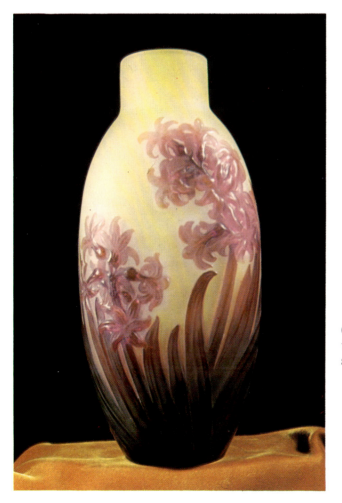

27

Gallé. 12" tall. Hyacinths decorate this mold blown vase which was subjected to two acid cuttings.

28

Gallé. 10″ tall. This rhododendron decoration was produced in this three layer mold blown glass vase with three acid cuttings.

29

Gallé. 13¾″ tall. The blossoms produced in this mold blown vase with acid cuttings strongly suggest an oriental influence in the decoration. (In private collection).

30

(A) Gallé. 9½" tall. Clematis blossoms and vine decorate this mold blown and acid cut vase. (In private collection).

(B) Gallé. 9" tall. Almost identical vase to that observed in "A" but in different colors.

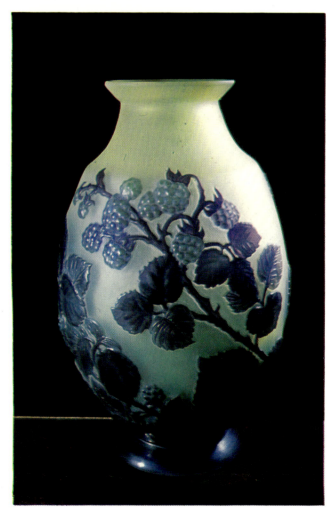

31

Gallé. 10" tall. In this mold blown vase only two acid cuttings were required to produce this raspberry decoration.

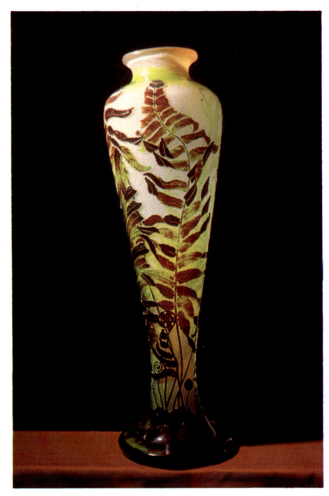

32

Gallé. 29½″ tall. This 18 lb. vase consists of four layers of glass. It has been subjected to three acid cuttings to produce this design of ferns from the forest floor of Lorraine. (Signature #40).

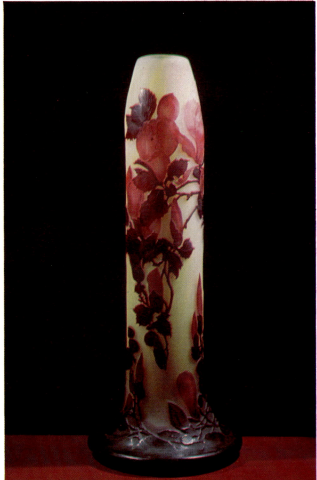

33

Gallé. This 28¼″ vase is beautifully decorated with cameo carving to produce this floral design. Weight: 20 lbs.

34

Gallé. 21″ tall. Three acid cuttings. There is a special stamp on the top surface of the base of this vase, the significance of which is uncertain, although it is probably a stamp placed there at the time of an exhibition.

35 (A) Gallé. 17½″ tall. Three acid cuttings were required to produce this lilac design. There is a special mark near the base of this vase which was apparently a mark placed on it at the time of exhibition and is the same mark which is present on the vase in illustration #34. (Signature #12).

(B) Gallé. 21″ tall. Same design and style of cutting as "A". (Signature #51).

36

Gallé. 12″ tall. This three layer cameo vase has three acid cuttings to produce this spider web design in the grapevine. (In the collection of Mr. and Mrs. Rex Cook).

37

A   B   C

(A) Gallé. 13½″ tall. Three acid cuttings. (Signature #41).

(B) Gallé. 9″ tall. Three acid cuttings. (Signature #42).

(C) Gallé. 10″ tall. Currants decorate this two layer Gallé vase which has been subjected to four acid cuttings. (Signature #52).

38

A   B   C

(A) Gallé. 14½″ tall. Unusual incised signature. Three layers of glass with three acid cuttings. (Signature #19).

(B) Gallé. 12½″ tall. Three acid cuttings were used to produce this chrysanthemum decoration in this four layer glass vase.

(C) Gallé. 12″ tall. Four layers of glass with three acid cuttings. The caramel-colored glass lining the inside of this vase was cut away behind the blossoms so this area of the foliage would be brighter. (Signature #31).

A   B   C

9 The vase in the center is slightly different in shape from the vases on each side, although all three have an almost identical shape.

(A) Gallé. 20″ tall. The glass layering and the design are essentially the same in this 13 lb. vase as in the one in illustration #32.

(B) Gallé. 19″ tall. This 8 lb. vase is the earliest of the three in this illustration. There is an interesting faint purplish iridescence in the center of the blossoms. (Signature #34).

(C) Gallé. 19½″ tall. This 14 lb. vase has three layers of glass and two acid cuttings to produce this floral design.

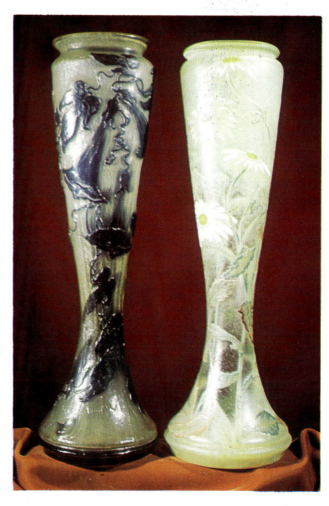

40 The same mold was used for these two vases to produce different styles in glass.

(A) Gallé. 23″ tall. Heavy acid cutting in the surface. Just below the cameo signature there is etched into the glass the word "Étude". (Signature #35).

(B) Gallé. 23″ tall. Acid cutting has produced the flowers in relief which have been decorated with enamels. The acid cutting has also produced the irregularly textured background surface in this vase. (Signature #36).

41

Gallé. 15½" tall. Four layers of glass with three acid cuttings produce this columbine decoration. (Signature #46).

42

(A) Gallé. 24½". The lotus lilly is carved in red on a greyish background. There are 19 red ribs in the base of this vase with 1[?] grooves throughout the body an[d] into the neck of this vase. Ther[e] is an unusual Gallé signature a[t] the top of the vase and beside th[e] signature is inscribed in came[o] relief the word "Bonheur". (Signature #60).

(B) Gallé. 26" tall. Only two aci[d] cuttings were required in thi[s] three layered cameo vase to pro[-]duce this floral design. (Signatur[e] #39).

43

(A) Gallé. 17" tall. Delphiniums are produced in cameo relief in this four layer glass vase.

(B) Gallé. 19" tall. Only two acid cuttings were required in this double layer vase to produce chrysanthemums in relief. (Signature #47).

(C) Gallé. 15½" tall. Three layers of glass with two acid cuttings.

A   B   C

44

(A) Gallé. 9″ tall. Five layers of glass with four acid cuttings were used to produce this clematis decoration. (Signature #63).

(B) Gallé. 6¾″ tall. Four layers of glass with three acid cuttings. (Signature #16).

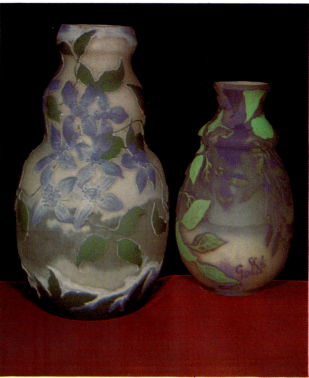

45

(A) Gallé. 16½″ tall. Five layers of glass with two acid cuttings. (Signature #45).

(B) Gallé. 14½″ tall. Hydrangia design is produced in this five layer glass vase with three acid cuttings.

46

(A) Gallé. 15″ tall. Five layers of glass with two acid cuttings produce this floral design. (Signature #37).

(B) Gallé. 17½″ tall. Five layers of glass with two acid cuttings also produce this floral design.

47 Gallé. This bowl is 4¼″ tall and 8¼″ in diameter. There are three layers of glass with two acid cuttings. Note the Gallé signature near the base which almost seems to be part of the floral design. (In the collection of Mr. and Mrs. William Arbeiter).

48 Gallé. 10″ tall. The streaks of colored glass in the background make this an unusual piece. (In the collection of Mr. and Mrs. William Arbeiter).

49 Gallé. 13″ tall. Three layers of glass with four acid cuttings. Note the streaked middle layer of glass which has been exposed to give the streaking within the petals of the blossoms. (In the collection of Mr. and Mrs. Rex Cook).

50

(A) Gallé. 12″ tall. Star signature. (Signature #61).

(B) Gallé. 6½″ tall. Three layers of glass with five acid cuttings.

(C) Gallé. 5½″ tall. Four layers of glass with four acid cuttings.

(D) Gallé. 5½″ tall. Four layers of glass with four acid cuttings. (Signature #9).

51

(A) Gallé. 8″ tall. Three layers of glass with four acid cuttings.

(B) Gallé. 10″ tall. Four layers of glass with four acid cuttings produce this hibiscus design.

(C) Gallé. 8½″ tall. Five layers of glass with four acid cuttings.

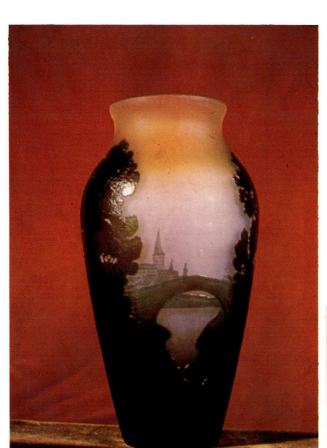

52
Gallé. 12″ tall. Five acid cuttings were used to produce this scenic vase. Hand work was required in the finishing process.

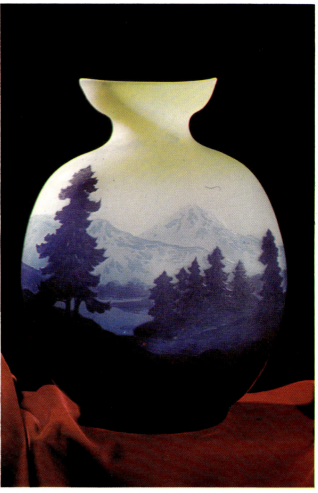

53
Gallé. 13″ tall. This unusually shaped vase has four layers of glass with four acid cuttings.

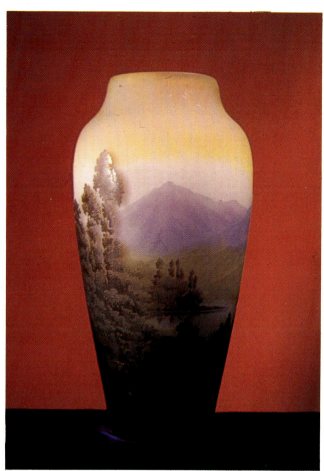

54 Gallé. 14″ tall. This multi-layer glass vase with finely acid-cut work has a star Gallé signature and therefore was produced after the death of Gallé. (Signature #62).

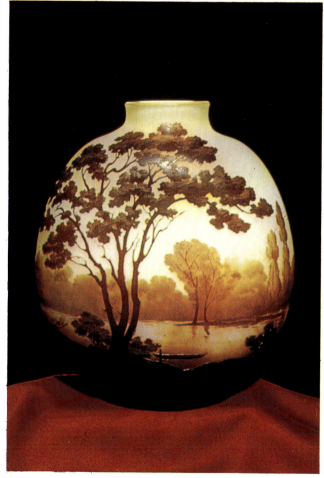

55 Gallé. 11″ tall. Four acid cuttings.

56

Gallé. 16½" tall. The body and base were blown separately. Only two acid cuttings were used to produce this scenic decoration.

57 Gallé. 8¾" tall. Three layers of glass with four acid cuttings.

58

Gallé. 16½" tall. Four acid cuttings were used in this vase of three layers of glass. (Signature #6).

59

Gallé. 15½" tall. Four acid cuttings. (Signature #11).

60 Gallé. 10" tall. Four acid cuttings were used in this multi-layer vase to produce this scene.

61

Gallé. 18" tall. Four layers of glass with three acid cuttings. This scenic vase is signed with the Gallé signature without a star; however, there is an inscription on the vase: "Souvenir de Marthe 1910". (In the collection of Mr. and Mrs. Rex Cook).

62

Gallé. This rose bowl is 7" ta[ll] and 8¼" in diameter. Four ac[id] cuttings.

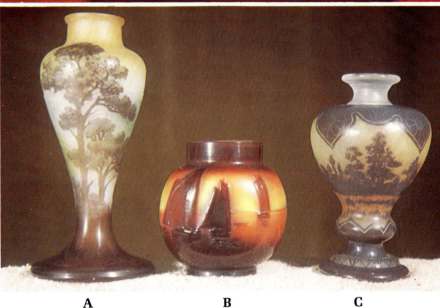

A   B   C

63

These scenic vases are all Gall[é]. There is acid cutting in all thes[e] vases with a moderate amount [of] hand finishing of "B", and wit[h] wheel sculpturing of the scen[ic] portion of "C".

(A) 6½" tall.

(B) 3¼" tall. (Signature #22).

(C) 5" tall. (Signature #27).

64

(A) Gallé. 10" tall. This scen[ic] Galle vase is divided into fiv[e] separate panels by tree trunk[s]. There are four layers of glass wit[h] three acid cuttings. Star signatur[e].

(B) Gallé. 12" tall. Sweet Willia[m] floral design produced in a fou[r] layer glass vase with three aci[d] cuttings.

65

Gallé. 3⅝" tall. 3¾" in diameter. This covered box has a molded pattern in the metal top matching the cameo decoration in the glass body of this box. (In private collection). (Signature #54).

66

Gallé. 3½" tall and 7" in maximum diameter. The base is composed of four layers of glass which has been cut into a scenic design. The top has four layers of glass and has 6 butterflies cut into the surface. Two metal dragonflies have been applied and each of these dragonflies has a hallmark.

67

(A) Gallé. 8" tall. This covered box with the mountain scene and the two birds soaring in the sky has three layers of glass in the body portion with four acid cuttings. The top has three layers of glass with two acid cuttings. (Signature #5).

(B) Gallé. 7" tall. This scenic egg-shaped covered box was made in three separate pieces with the base and bowl fused. There are three layers of glass in the bowl portion and in the top with two acid cuttings both in the scenic portion and in the top.

(C) Gallé. 8" tall. This evergreen decoration is produced in two layers of glass with two acid cuttings.

A   B   C

68

(A) Gallé. 14½″ tall.

(B) Gallé. 7½″ tall.

"A" is signed with the name Gallé with a star, whereas, "B" has a Gallé signature without a star. Both are considered to be production commercial ware and the piece without the star was likely also produced after Gallé's death.

69

Gallé. 13½″ tall. This multi-layer glass vase was subjected to several acid cuttings. (In the collection of Mr. and Mrs. William Arbeiter).

70

Gallé. 15½" tall. (In the collection of Mr. and Mrs. William Arbeiter).

71

Gallé. 8¼" tall. There are three layers of glass in this vase with the base glass being clear. (In the collection of Mr. and Mrs. William Arbeiter). (Signature #56).

72 **(A)** Gallé. This roughly triangular bowl is 10″ in maximum dimension and has acid-cut cameo design in both internal and external surfaces.

(B) Gallé. This bowl is 3½″ tall and 9½″ in diameter.

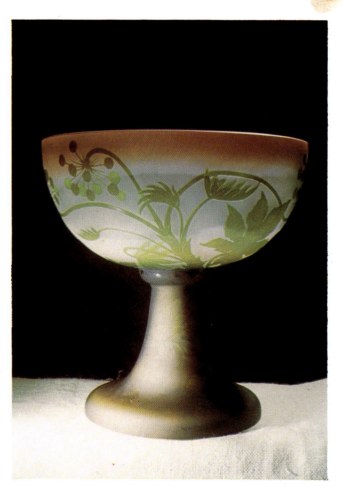

73 Gallé. This punch bowl appears deceptively small in this photograph. Height is 15″ and the bowl portion is 14¾″ in diameter. The bowl holds over two and one-half gallons of liquid. This punch bowl weighs 20 pounds. There is a star signature. (In the collection of Mr. Ray Keller).

A   B   C
         D

74

(A) Gallé. This bottle is 7½″ tall. Three layers of glass with two acid cuttings were used to produce this spring wild flower design. (Signature #4).

(B) Gallé. 5″ tall. Oak design with acorns produced with two acid cuttings. (Signature #8).

(C) Gallé. This bowl is 4″ in diameter and 3¾″ tall. Three layers of glass with two acid cuttings.

(D) Gallé. 2¼″ tall. 4½″ in diameter. Fern design. Star signature. Three glass layers with three acid cuttings.

75

(A) Gallé. 5½″ tall. Carnation design produced with two acid cuttings.

(B) Gallé. 4½″ tall. This spheroid vase is converted to a night light by the application of the metal top which has a light fixture within it. Three layers of glass with two acid cuttings.

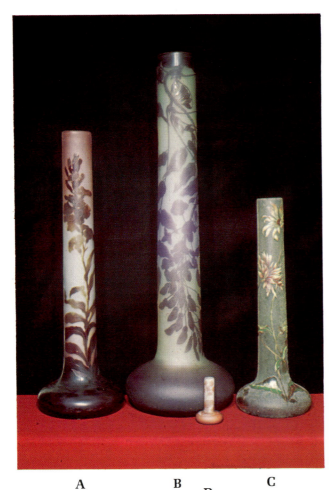

76

(A) Gallé. 23½" tall. This vase weighs 8 lbs.

(B) Gallé. This stick vase is 30" tall and weighs 17 lbs.

(C) This Gallé vase is 17¾" tall. This vase was blown from amber glass with acid cutting in the surface outlining the flowers in relief. The flowers were then enameled and decorated with gold. The background has a rough finish produced by acid cutting. (Signature #49).

(D) This small Gallé stick vase is 3½" tall, has two glass layers and has a nasturtium design. This is included to give a better appreciation of the relative size of these vases. This small stick vase is also included in photograph #85.

77

Gallé. These seven stick vases range between 13½" and 23½" in height. (Signature #38 was copied from vase "F").

78

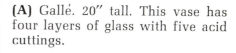

(A) Gallé. 20″ tall. This vase has four layers of glass with five acid cuttings.

(B) Gallé. 20″ tall. Four layers of glass with only two acid cuttings produce this fern design. (Signature #10).

79 (A) Gallé. 24″ tall. This foliage design is produced in a vase with five glass layers and three acid cuttings. Vase weighs 13 lbs.

(B) Gallé. 22″ tall. This iris design was also produced in a vase with five glass layers and three acid cuttings. The deep white layer is rather unusual in French cameo glass. 9 lbs.

80

(A) Gallé. 8½″ tall. (See signature #13). (In the collection of Mrs. Frances Craig).

(B) Gallé. 7″ tall.

81

Gallé.

(A) 6¾" tall.

(B) 4¼" in diameter. 2" tall. Within the clear glass are 25 ribs of green glass extending from the central portion of the base into the top edge of the bowl. There is acid cut cameo relief of flowers and there is also acid cut intaglio outlining of some portions of the design. Enamel decoration was then added.

(C) This 2" amber glass might be properly included as there are some thistles and geometric designs outlined in the surface in cameo relief with some gold and enamel decoration.

(D) This small wine glass is 3" tall and the bowl portion is 1¾" in diameter. The floral pattern in the silver base matches that of the cameo design in the bowl. In the glass portion there is some enameling in addition to acid cutting. (Signature #57).

(E) 3¾" tall. (Signature #18).

(F) 4½" tall. (Signature #2).

(G) 5" tall.

82

Gallé.

(A) 9½" tall.

(B) 8" tall.

(C) 8" tall.

(D) 5" tall. (Signature #29)

(E) 4¾" tall. (Signature #14).

(F) 5" tall.

83

(A) Gallé. 8" tall. Note the grasshopper and the unusual signature. (Signature #21).

(B) Gallé. 5½" tall. The two butterflies decorate the elongated neck of this vase over the water lilly decoration.

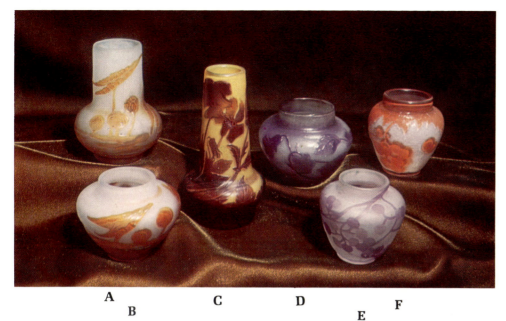

84.

Gallé.

(A) 4″ tall.

(B) 2½″ tall. (Signature #64).

(C) 5″ tall.

(D) 3″ tall.

(E) 2½″ tall.

(F) 2½″ tall.

85.

Gallé. The 7 small vases range between 3½″ and 4″ tall. The small whiskey ("shot") glass measures 2″ tall.

86.

Gallé.

(A) This circular bowl is 2½″ deep and 6″ in diameter, is decorated with the Mayflower, and has an infolding of one side.

(B) This bowl is 3¼″ tall and 6″ in diameter with orchid design.

(C) This bowl is 4½″ tall, 6″ in diameter.

(D) This vase with water lily design is 9½″ tall. (Signature #3).

(E) 6″ tall.

(F) 6″ tall. (See signature #7).

65

This photograph is included to give a better appreciation of the relative sizes. Each of these pieces is presented in subsequent pictures.

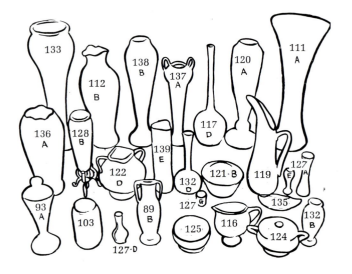

Numbers in the accompanying diagram refer to the photograph in which the piece is illustrated.

This photograph is included to give a better appreciation of the relative sizes. Each of these pieces is presented in subsequent pictures.

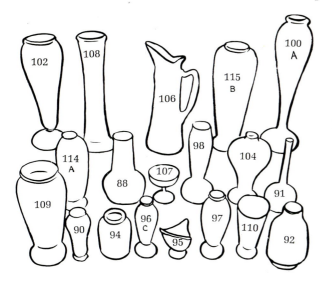

Numbers in the accompanying diagram refer to the photograph in which the piece is illustrated.

67

87.

Daum. 12½″ tall. Bowl is 6½″ in diameter. The outstanding feature of this piece is the finely carved figures about the bowl. (In the collection of Mr. and Mrs. Don Williams). (Signature #78).

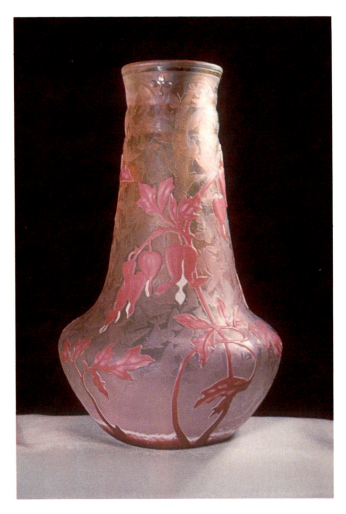

88.

Daum. 10½″ tall. Dated 1895. Three layers of glass. The background in this piece has many butterflies cut into the surface. The foliage was grossly outlined by acid cutting and was then sculptured using wheel engraving. (Signature #93).

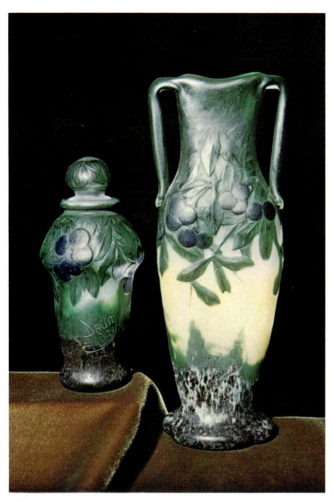

89.

An unusual Daum style in two unusually shaped pieces.

(A) 6½" tall. The work in the bottle and stopper has been performed using wheel cutting.

(B) 10" tall. Wheel engraving has also been used to produce the design in this vase. (Signature #79).

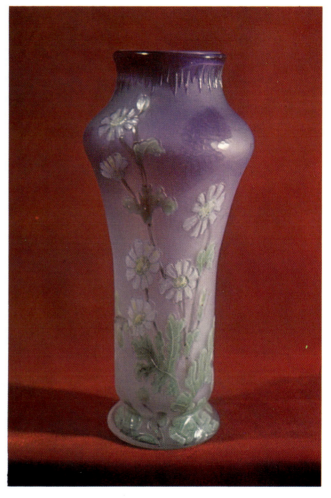

90.

Daum. 7½" tall. The floral design is trapped between layers of clear glass. There is sculptured cameo cutting in the clear glass over the incorporated floral design. There is also some wheel cutting in the frosted surface in several areas to give a "hammered metal" appearance.

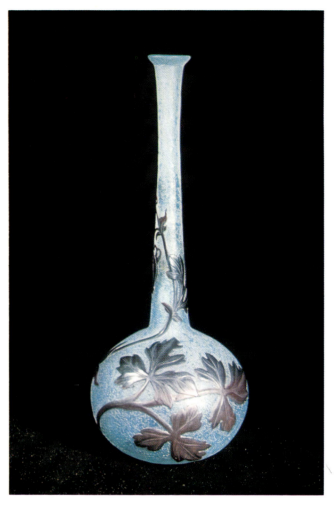

91.

Daum. 11″ tall. The gross outline of the floral design in this vase was made using acid cutting techniques; however, the floral portion was then sculptured using wheel cutting. (Signature #71).

92.

Daum. 9″ tall. There are four figures on this vase, two old ladies and two old gentlemen. Note the cross of Lorraine is cut into many areas throughout the background. (Signature #70).

93.

(A) Daum. 11½″ tall. (Signature #90).

(B) 7½″ tall. (Signature #88).

94.

Daum. 6½″ tall. The leaves and stems in this foliage were cut using acid; however, the buds and blossoms were sculptured using wheel cutting. (Signature #82).

95.

Daum. 4½″ tall. The buds and blossoms were sculptured by wheel cutting.

96.

Daum. All of the foliage in these three vases have some wheel sculpturing and backgrounds of these vases have acid cut designs.

(A) 9¼″ tall. Design in the metal base matches the cameo floral design.

(B) 8¼″ tall. Design in the metal base matches the cameo design.

(C) 8½″ tall.

97.

Daum. 10″ tall. The crocuses outlined in this piece were acid cut; however, there is some wheel cutting in the background to produce the "hammered metal" appearance. (Signature #91).

98.

Daum. 12" tall. Background shows a "hammered metal" appearance which has been produced by wheel cutting. The crocus blossoms and stems have been applied after the vase was formed and after the blank was layered. These portions of applied glass were then sculptured using wheel cutting techniques.

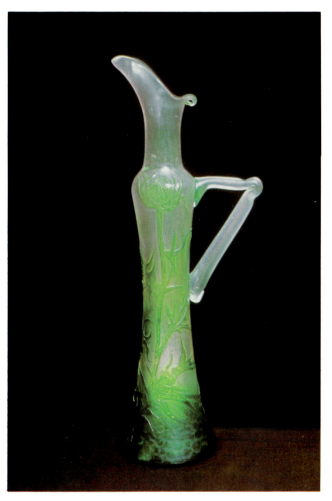

99.

Daum. 16" tall. There is some wheel sculpturing evident both in the surface background and in the foliage in this pitcher. (In the collection of Mr. and Mrs. Rex Cook).

100.

(A) Daum. 20″ tall. There is wheel sculpturing of all of the foliage in this piece and the "hammered metal" appearance in the background was produced by wheel cutting. (Signature #74).

(B) Daum. 20″ tall. The cameo thistle pattern in this piece was produced by acid cutting with wheel cutting throughout the background to produce the "hammered metal" appearance. (Signature #73).

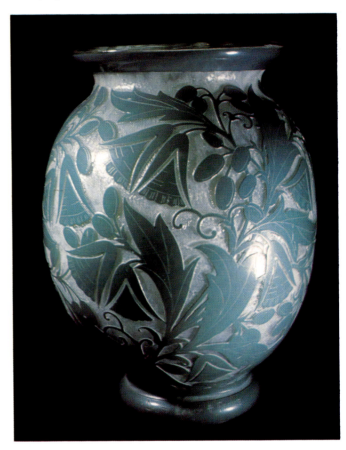

101.

Daum. 16″ tall. Two acid cuttings. This large vase weighs 22 lbs. (In the collection of Mr. and Mrs. William Arbeiter).

102.

Daum. 15½″ tall. The blossoms were sculptured with wheel cutting. The remainder of cameo relief in this vase was produced with acid cutting. (Signature #94).

103.

Daum. 7″ tall. Clear glass has been acid cut and painted. Note the Japanese influence in the decoration. This piece is signed Daum Nancy France with the cross of Lorraine. (Signature #89).

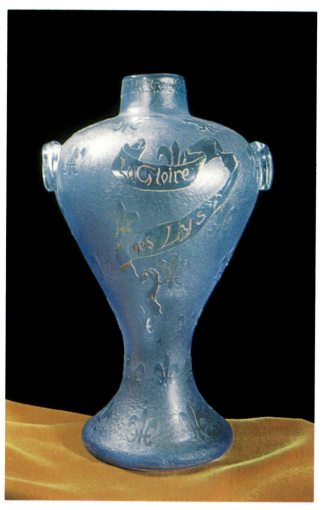

104.

Daum. 11″ tall. Clear blue glass has been acid cut and frosted in portions with a fleur-de-lis cameo design in the surface. Across the front there is a ribbon bearing the inscription "La Gloire des Lys". Note the applied flat handles at the sides of this vase.

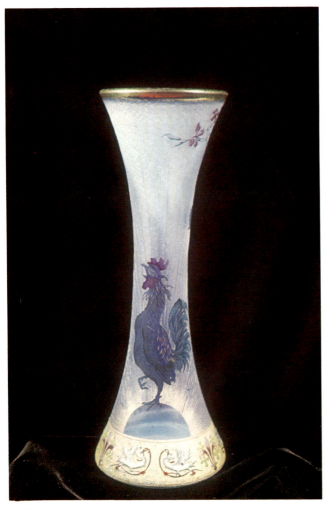

105.

Daum. 15⅞" tall. Acid cut and then decorated in a style which is rather typical for much of Daum's fine decorating. (In the collection of Mr. and Mrs. William Arbeiter).

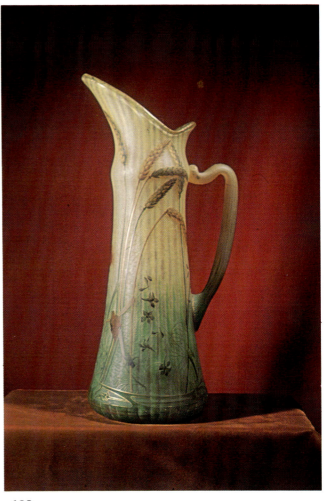

106.

Daum. 17" tall. The wheat, violet, and poppy outlines were produced by acid cutting, and the relief areas were then decorated in a style which is rather typically that of Daum. There are 32 streaks of green glass extending from the central portion of the base into the mid-portion of the body. There are also 32 streaks of tan glass which extend from the base into the uppermost portion of this pitcher. About the upper half of this pitcher, there are 16 streaks of gold-colored glass interspersed between the tan colored glass streaks. There are also streaks of glass within the handle which are quite narrow but which correspond in color to those found in the body of the pitcher.

107

Daum. This champagne glass is 4½" tall. The bowl portion is composed of clear glass with some yellow glass incorporated into the central portion. The stem and vase are cased in green glass over clear with some mottled green and yellow within this clear glass. The outside surface of the entire piece has been acid cut and beautifully decorated. Beneath the rooster is the word "Vigilat". Inscribed around the lip of the glass is "XIII Concours National et International de Tir. Nancy 1906". About the base is a quotation "Qui s'y Frotte s'y Pique."

108

Daum. 17½" tall. Acid cut surface and decorated. There are 3 green and 2 red "jeweled" areas in the surface of this vase produced by applying glass to the surface while the blank was still hot. The geometric style of decoration about the base and lower portion of the vase is seen in a number of pieces produced by Daum. Note the mottled work in the base glass which was produced by the glass blower and which adds to the beauty of this vase.

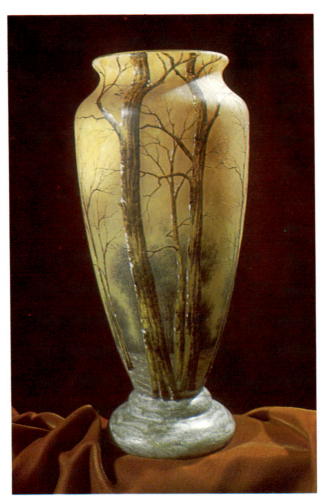

109.

Daum. 13½" tall. The winter scene produced by acid cutting and enameling is one of Daum's most popular designs. (Signature #77).

110.

Daum. 8" tall. This fall scene was produced by acid cutting and enameling, and is less frequently encountered than are the winter scene pieces. (Signature #76).

111.

All four of these vases are Daum.

(A) 19½" tall. Three layers of glass and three acid cuttings were used to produce this scenic vase. (Signature #85).

(B) 11½" tall. Three layers of glass with three acid cuttings.

(C) 5½" tall. Three layers of glass with three acid cuttings.

(D) 8" tall. There are three layers of glass with a single acid cutting. The surface was then decorated to give this detailed fall scene.

112. **(A)** Daum. 16½" tall. Four acid cuttings.

(B) Daum. 15½" tall. Four acid cuttings.

113.

All eight of these vases are Daum.

(A) 5" tall. Three layers of glass with three acid cuttings.

(B) Bowl is 2½" tall and 6" in diameter. Surface is acid cut and decorated. (Signature #80).

(C) 4½" tall. Three layers of glass with three acid cuttings.

(D) 4" tall. Three layers of glass with four acid cuttings and with some wheel cutting in the surface.

(E) 4" tall. Surface is acid cut and decorated. This is not a true cameo piece as the design is painted rather than in cameo relief.

(F) 3½" tall. Three layers of glass with acid cut surface and decorated.

(G) 8" tall. Acid cut surface and decorated. The initials "AR" follow the Daum signature. (Signature #86).

(H) 3½" tall. Three layers of glass with deeply cut surface with three acid cuttings.

114.

Daum. Both of these mold blown vases are 11½" tall. There are three layers of glass with the outside and inside layers both mottled. There are two acid cuttings and the scenic detail is finished with wheel cutting. (Signature #92 copied from vase "B").

115.

Daum. Each of these vases is 16" tall. Both are mold blown vases in the same style as those in illustration #114. These vases were made in a variety of colors including pink and white, in addition to the two pictured here.

116.

Daum. 6″ tall. There is acid cutting in the surface to produce this water scene with ships. (Signature #83).

117.

All four of these vases are Daum.

(A) 8¾″ tall. Three layers of glass with three acid cuttings.

(B) 4″ tall. The technique for producing this winter scene is the same as that for the small piece in this photograph.

(C) 1″ tall. This winter scene was produced by acid cutting followed by decorating.

(D) 16½″ tall. Four layers of glass with three acid cuttings.

118.

Daum. 6″ tall. This acid cut and decorated pitcher is in the same style scene as the "D" vase in illustration #111.

119.

Daum. 15" tall. Geraniums produced by two acid cuttings in this three layer glass pitcher. Note the slight iridescence in the surface of the handle.

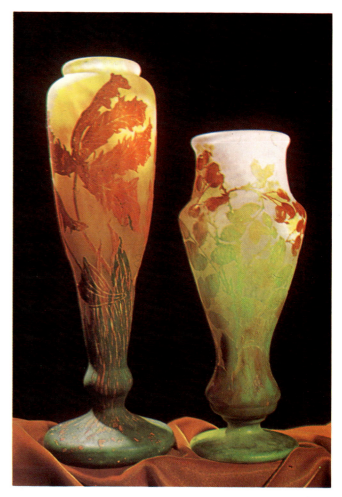

120.

(A) Daum. 16¾" tall. There are two acid cuttings to produce this cameo design.

(B) Daum. 13" tall. Two acid cuttings produce this cameo design of this wild rose after blossoming with the seed pods well demonstrated.

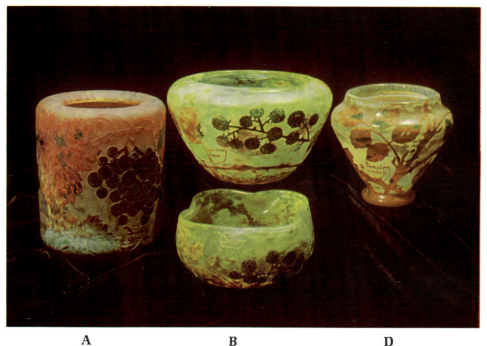

A   B   D
         C

121.

All four of these vases are Daum.

(A) 6″ tall. Grape pattern.

(B) Bowl is 4″ tall with raspberry pattern.

(C) This bowl is 2½″ tall and 5″ in maximum diameter with raspberry pattern. (Signature #81).

(D) 4″ tall. Thorny vine with leaves.

122.

Daum.

(A) 14″ tall. Acid cut and decorated. There are three honey bees in the band about the area of the junction of the neck with the body of this vase.

(B) 10½″ tall. Single acid cutting with nasturtium design.

(C) Circular bowl is 5″ tall and 7½″ in maximum diameter. Single acid cutting.

(D) This two-handled bowl is 7″ tall. Single acid cutting with floral design and 8 butterflies about the upper portion.

123.

Daum. Covered box is 3½" tall. Two applied cabochons are present on the lid, both carved into the form of beetles. Another jeweled cabochon is applied to one side of the bowl. There are three layers of glass with a single acid cutting.

124.

Daum. 4½" tall. Surface was acid cut and then subjected to some wheel cutting before decorating.

125.

Daum. This covered box is 4″ tall. The jonquil blossoms have been applied by technique known as "padding" and this applied glass then has been sculptured to produce the blossoms. The remainder of the covered box has had cameo relief produced by acid cutting.

126.

(A) Daum. 4½″ tall. This covered box in peacock feather design has acid cutting in the surface. The central portion of each of the peacock feathers has a purple and blue coloring produced by insets of glass which were placed into the surface of the blank while it was still hot. The design, placed on the surface of this blank before acid cutting, was made so that the peacock feathers conform to the locations of these glass insets.

(B) 7″ tall. This vase has a peacock feather design as in "A" and is produced in the same manner.

C　　　D　　A　　E　　F　　B　　G

127.

Daum. All seven of these pieces are produced by acid cutting technique with decorating in a style which was well developed by and rather typical of Daum.

(A) Two handled bowl. 3¼″ tall and 7″ in length. The orchid decoration is in enamel with a finely acid-cut spider web in the background.

(B) 2¾″ tall. Red clover decoration.

(C) 7″ tall. Bleeding hearts in cameo relief decorate this vase with the phrase "Mon Cour Auvez" carved around the base. This vase is made of clear glass with a thin layer of blue glass layered on the inside surface.

(D) 5″ tall. Poppy design.

(E) 4¼″ tall. Lily design.

(F) 2½″ tall. Both the top and the bowl of this covered box are signed and have a fuchsia decoration.

(G) The decoration in this 1¾″ tall whiskey glass is the same as in the covered box by which it stands.

128.

(A) Daum. 14½″ tall. Acid cut and decorated.

(B) Daum. 12¾″ tall. Acid cut with fuchsia decoration. Metal mounting.

129

Daum. Both pitchers are acid cut and decorated.

(A) 3″ tall with violet decoration.

(B) 3¾″ tall with corn flower decoration.

130

Daum. All seven pieces are acid cut and decorated.

(A) 4¼″ tall, poppy design.

(B) 4¾″ tall, violet design.

(C) 4¼″ tall, fuchsia design.

(D) Tumbler is 5″ tall with cornflower design.

(E) Tumbler, 4¾″ tall, sweet pea design.

(F) Tumbler, 4¼″ tall, orchid design with finely cut spider web in the background.

(G) 4½″ tall, dandelion design with cameo cut phrase, "Comme au vent la plume."

131.

All are from 1″ to 3½″ tall. These ten small Daum pieces are all acid cut and decorated. The miniature ice bucket in the front center which is white with black decoration has acid cutting in its surface but is not properly classified as cameo since the decorated areas are not in cameo relief. This piece has the same type work as that noted in #113-E.

87

132

These four vases are all Daum.

(A) 8¼″ tall.

(B) 7¼″ tall.

(C) 6¾″ tall. Acid cut with gold gilt decoration.

(D) 10″ tall. Acid cut with black enamel and gold decoration. (Signature #72).

133.

Daum. 18½″ tall. This vase with ginko tree decoration is without a bottom and was not made for flowers, but as a container in which to display peacock feathers which were popular as decorative items at the time this vase was made.

134.

Daum. 12″ in diameter. Nasturtium in cameo relief. (In the collection of Mr. and Mrs. Rex Cook).

135.

Daum. This small boat-shaped vase is 1½" tall and 6½" in length. The bleeding hearts were carved in the pink glass which was applied to the surface of the blank after it was formed.

136

Daum.

(A) 13½" tall. Three layers of glass. Glass forming the blossoms and portions of the buds was worked into the surface while the blank was still hot. The foliage was grossly outlined by a single acid cutting. Buds, blossoms, leaves, and stems were then carved using the engraving wheel with the best carving in the four large blossoms.

(B) 8½" tall. Four layers of glass with three acid cuttings.

(C) Ovoid bowl measuring 11½" by 7½" in greater and lesser dimensions. 3½" tall. Single acid cutting and decorated.

(D) Circular bowl. 8½" in maximum diameter. Single acid cutting with wheel engraving of the foliage.

137

Daum.

(A) 14½" tall. There are three glass layers with three acid cuttings. Note the beetle cut into the base of this piece.

(B) 16¾" tall. The design was produced in this four layer cameo vase with four acid cuttings. (Signature #75).

138.

These five vases are all Daum.

(A) 15½″ tall. Acid cut and decorated. Clear glass with white inside layer.

(B) 16¾″ tall. Acid cut surface. Blossoms were wheel sculptured in glass which was applied after the blank was formed. Remainder of surface cutting was with acid.

(C) 20″ tall. Wild iris decorates this four layer cameo vase.

(D) 19″ tall. This two handled vase has been subjected to acid cutting; however, the floral portion has been sculptured with wheel engraving.

(E) 18″ tall. Three acid cuttings produce this cockscomb cameo design.

139.

Daum.

(A) 11″ tall. Three layers of glass with two acid cuttings. Wheel sculpturing of blossoms.

(B) 11½″ tall. Two glass layers. Single acid cutting and decorated.

(C) 11¾″ tall. Acid cut surface with wheel sculpturing of daisies followed by gold decorating.

(D) 9¼″ tall. Cockscomb cameo design in four layer glass vase with three acid cuttings.

(E) 11″ tall. Decorating is with same technique as in "B" in a vase of different shape and coloring.

(F) 12″ tall. Same coloring and style of work as in "A" with wheel cut buds and blossoms.

140.

Daum.

(A) 14½" tall. The glass bowl was subjected to a single acid cutting on its external surface which was then decorated. The cameo bowl is supported by the metal figure which in turn is on a marble base.

(B) 14" tall. The three cameo glass shades and the metal mounting were initially part of a chandelier. There was a 12½" diameter cameo bowl which was also a part of this chandelier. The metal supporting structure was reshaped and mounted on a small marble base to make a desk lamp.

141.

Daum bowl. 4½" tall. 8¾" in diameter. Acid cut and decorated. Metal base.

142.

Daum.

(A) 3¼" tall. Glass box with metal top, both of which have a poppy design. Top is hallmarked.

(B) 5¾" long. Spirit bottle with cameo strawberry design in the glass. Removable metal at the base serves as a small cup. Top is hallmarked.

(C) Scent bottle, 3" tall. Hinged top with mistletoe design in the top and cameo mistletoe design in the glass base. Cameo work also in the glass stopper which has been placed beside the bottle in the photograph.

(D) Scent bottle. 7½" tall. The metal top has several perforations beneath which there is a wick which extends down into the body of the bottle. (Signature #87).

This photograph is included to give a better appreciation of the relative sizes. Each of these pieces is presented in subsequent pictures.

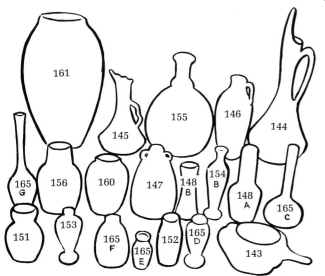

Numbers in the accompanying diagram refer to the photograph in which the piece is illustrated.

143.

Muller Croismare. 5" tall. 11" long including handle. This eerie, wooded scene has an owl on one side, and a wolf's head on the top which is in the form of an applied glass cabochon. On the back side there is a large bat flying through the woods. Signature is in cameo relief in the base.

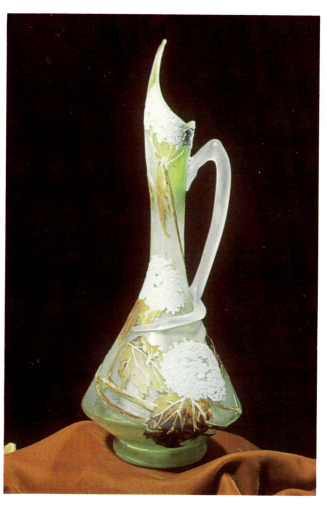

144.
Muller. This pitcher is 19" tall. The hydrangea design is produced in cameo relief with some painting of the leaves and stems.

145.

Muller Croismare. This rustic pitcher is 10" tall. Two cabochons carved into the form of beetles are present on the leaves. Note that the glass surface has the appearance of that seen on ancient glass. (Signature #97).

146.

Muller Fres Luneville. 10½" tall. Raspberry bush is outlined in cameo relief with some painting of the foliage. (Signature #103).

147.

Muller. This two handled vase is 8½" tall. The body of the snail and several of the leaves in this piece are formed by glass applied to the surface after the initial blank was blown. (Signature #100).

148.

(A) Muller Fres Luneville. 9" tall.

(B) Muller. 6½" tall. Note the withered vine and berries in this winter scene. (Signature #99).

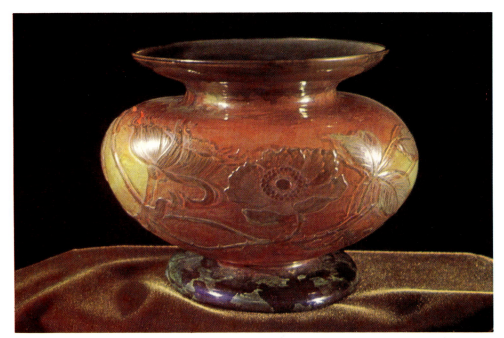

149.

Muller. 6″ tall. Wheel sculpturing in the cameo design. (In the collection of Mr. and Mrs. William Arbeiter).

150.

Muller Croismare. 5″ tall. Note intaglio cutting as well as cameo in this piece. (In the collection of Mr. and Mrs. William Arbeiter).

151

Muller Croismare. 6″ tall. Both acid cutting and wheel engraving are evident in the cameo work in this piece. (Signature #98).

152.

Muller Croismare. 6″ tall. The fine quality of cutting in this piece was accomplished with wheel engraving.

153.

Muller Croismare. 6½″ tall. The background has been cut away largely by acid with most of the work in the flowers accomplished by wheel engraving. (Signature #101).

154.

All three of these pieces have had the background cut away using acid and the flowers have been carved using wheel cutting.

(A) Muller Croismare. 6½″ tall.

(B) Croismare. 8½″ tall. (Signature #102).

(C) Muller Croismare. 6½″ tall. (Signature #96).

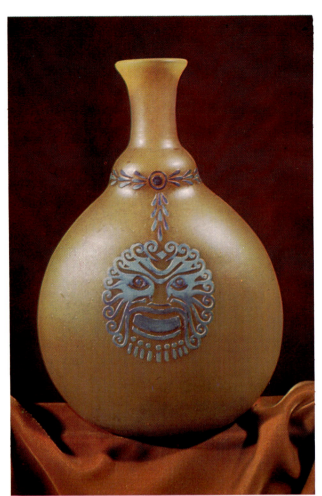

155.

Muller Fres Luneville. 12½" tall. This vase has five layers of glass. The same mask design is present in both the front and back sides of this vase. Included with the Muller signature is "Atepier Primavera."

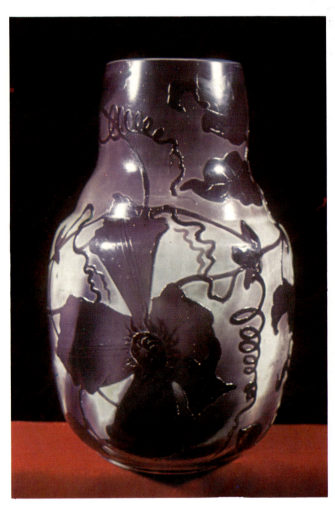

156.

Muller Croismare. 8" tall. Four layers of glass, two acid cuttings. (Signature #95).

157.

Croismare. 10⅝" tall. Note that the scene is produced by cameo cutting except for the snake which is intaglio. (In the collection of Mr. and Mrs. William Arbeiter).

158.

Muller. 6½″ tall. Four acid cuttings. (In the collection of Mr. and Mrs. William Arbeiter).

159.

Muller. 12¾″ tall. Note the poppy blossoms are shiny whereas the remainder of the vase has a frosted finish. Four acid cuttings. (In the collection of Mr. and Mrs. William Arbeiter).

160.

Muller Fres Luneville. 7″ tall. Five layers of glass, five acid cuttings. (Signature #104).

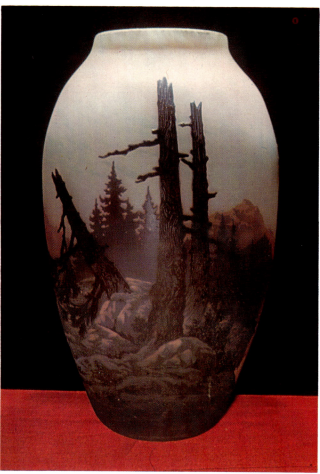

161 & 162.

Muller Frēres Luneville. The two photographs above illustrate the front and back side of a Muller vase measuring 16″ in height. There are four layers of glass with four acid cuttings. The streaks, scarcely visible in the upper portion of the vase, represent clouds and are not demonstrated well in the photograph. Note the intaglio cutting for the waterfall in photograph #161. This is a well-planned and well-executed piece of cameo glass using acid cutting. In many pieces both the front and back sides have almost equally attractive cameo work. (Signature #105).

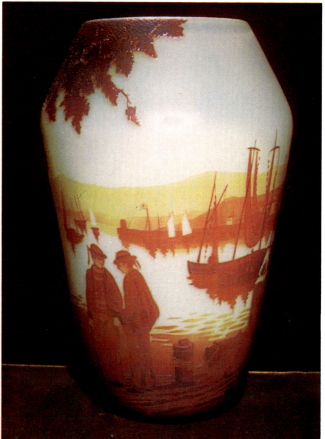

163.

Muller Fres Luneville. 17″ tall. This interesting scenic vase was formed from a blank with five glass layers with four acid cuttings. There are five people produced in cameo relief.
(In the collection of Mr. and Mrs. Rex Cook).

164.

Muller. 12″ tall. Five acid cuttings. (In the collection of Mr. and Mrs. Larry Wood).

165.

All seven pieces in this photograph are signed Muller Fres Luneville.

(A) 6″ tall. Seven birds are in cameo relief.

(B) 3½″ tall. Bowl portion is 6½″ in diameter. Note the dragonflies among the weeping willows.

(C) 10″ tall. Again a dragonfly is pictured among weeping willows.

(D) 5½″ tall.

(E) 4″ tall. Note the children at play in this scenic vase.

(F) 6″ tall.

(G) 11½″ tall.

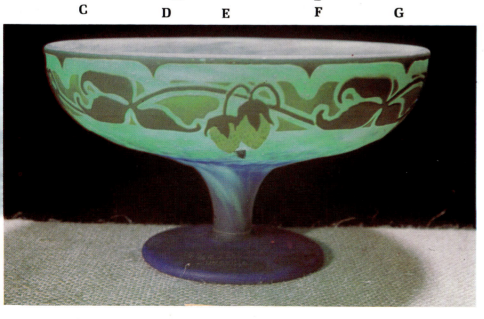

166.

Muller Fres Luneville. 4½″ tall. Bowl portion is 8″ in diameter.

This photograph is included to give a better appreciation of the relative sizes. Each of these pieces is presented in subsequent pictures.

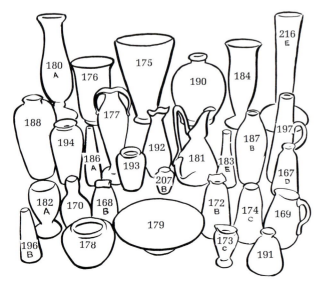

Numbers in the accompanying diagram refer to the photograph in which the piece is illustrated.

This photograph is included to give a better appreciation of the relative sizes. Each of these pieces is presented in subsequent pictures.

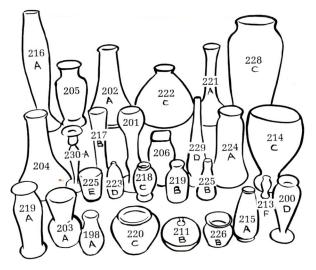

Numbers in the accompanying diagram refer to the photograph in which the piece is illustrated.

103

167.

(A) Legras. 8½" tall. Geometric design in cameo and intaglio with both shiny and frosted finish. (Signature #107).

(B) Legras. 6" tall. Acid cut and painted.

(C) Legras. 12½" tall. Snails are incorporated in the geometric design about the lower half of this vase, and the acid cut portion was then painted.

(D) Legras. 8" tall. Acid cut relief design which is painted.

168.

(A) Legras. 4½" tall. Two layers of glass in the vase which has been acid cut and painted.

(B) Legras. 7½" tall. Four layers of glass have been subjected to four acid baths to produce this scenic cameo design.

(C) 4" tall. Single layer of glass has been acid cut and painted.

169.

Legras. 8″ tall. Four layers of glass were subjected to three acid baths to produce the cameo relief in this pitcher.

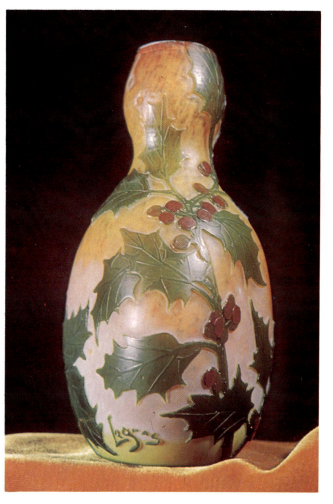

170.

Legras. 8″ tall. There are six separate layers of glass in this vase. Two acid cuttings produce the cameo relief and the holly berries were painted. (Signature #108).

171.

These two rather large vases show the usual style of deVez in two different types of subjects.

(A) 19½″ tall. Four layers of glass with three acid cuttings. (In the collection of Mr. and Mrs. Rex Cook).

(B) 17½″ tall. (In the collection of Mrs. Dorothy Galley).

172.

These two vases also demonstrate the deVez style. Figures of persons are relatively unusual in French cameo pieces.

(A) 12″ tall. (Signature #111).

(B) 9″ tall. (Signature #114).

173.

(A) deVez. 6" tall. This vase has three glass layers and was subjected to three acid cuttings.

(B) deVez. 3½" tall. Three acid cuttings.

(C) deVez. 5½" tall. Only two acid cuttings were required to produce this detailed scenic cameo vase. (Signature #110).

174.

deVez.

(A) 16" tall. Three layers of glass with three acid cuttings. Note the slight iridescence and the strong similarity in style to those in photograph #207. (In the collection of Mr. and Mrs. Rex Cook).

(B) 8" tall. Three glass layers with two acid cuttings. (In the collection of Mr. and Mrs. Rex Cook).

(C) 8½" tall. Four glass layers with three acid cuttings.

175.

Delatte. 14″ tall. Four acid cuttings were used to produce this floral decoration.

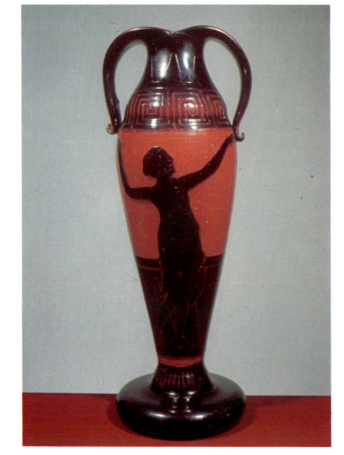

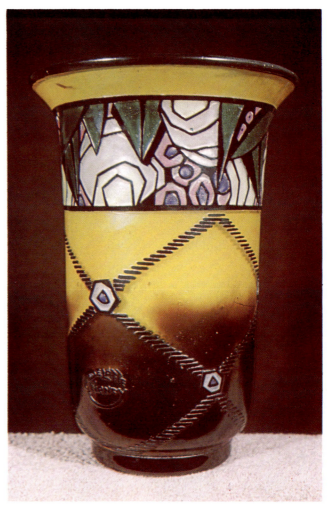

176.

Delatte. 10½″ tall. Three layers of glass. Design is produced by a single acid cutting followed by enamel decoration. (Signature #109).

177.

Delatte. 14¾″ tall. Three layers of glass with two acid cuttings. There is an almost identical figure on both front and back. The manner in which the handles were formed from a portion of the top of the vase is also of interest in this piece.

178.

Delatte. 5½" tall. Four moths adorn this two layer cameo bowl which has a combined frosted and shiny finish.

179.

Delatte. 4" tall. Bowl portion has 12" diameter. There are five moths on the upper surface in cameo relief. On the undersurface of the bowl portion, there are eight moths in intaglio. Portions of four of the moths in the upper surface are brighter because some of the darker glass has been cut away in the undersurface of the bowl portion.

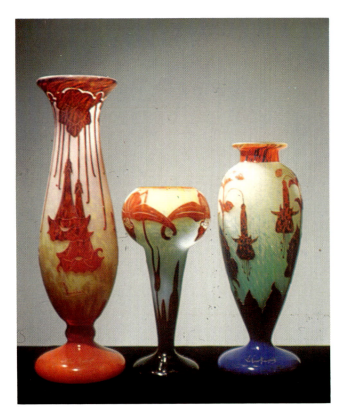

180.

Le Verre Francais.

(A) 14″ tall. Also signed "Charder" in cameo in the body of the vase. (Signature #116).

(B) 8″ tall. (Signature #113).

(C) 11½″ tall. (Signature #117).

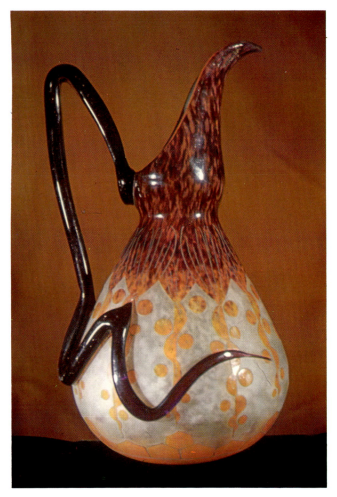

181.

Le Verre Francais. 12½″ tall. Single acid cutting.

182.

Le Verre Francais.

(A) 8″ tall. Also signed "Charder" in cameo on the body of the vase.

(B) 5½″ tall. Etched signature at the base. Also small bit of "candy cane" glass impressed into base as identifying mark. (Signature #115).

(C) 7″ tall. Signed only with the "candy cane" glass mark in the base.

183.

Richard.

(A) This bowl is 3″ tall and 5½″ in diameter. Three layers of glass with two acid cuttings.

(B) 4″ tall.

(C) 7½″ tall. Only two acid cuttings were required to produce this iris design.

(D) 8½″ tall. (Signature #121).

(E) 9″ tall. This wild orchid design was produced in this two layered vase with two acid cuttings. (Signature #122).

184.

Richard. 13½″ tall. Two acid cuttings were used to produce this grapevine design.

185.

D'Argental. 4″ tall. This scene was produced from a blank of two layers of glass with three acid baths. (Signature #119).

186.

(A) D'Argental. 9½″ tall. This detailed scene was produced from a blank with two glass layers with three acid cuttings.

(B) D'Argental. 9½″ tall. The blank for this piece was identical to that for "A"; however, in this piece, a thistle design was produced with two acid baths.

187.

D'Argental.

(A) 10″ tall. This interesting rose design was produced from a blank of two glass layers with three acid cuttings.

(B) 11¼″ tall. Two glass layers. Two acid cuttings.

(C) 11½″ tall. Two glass layers with three acid cuttings.

188.

D'Argental. 13″ tall. Two layers of glass. Two acid cuttings.

113

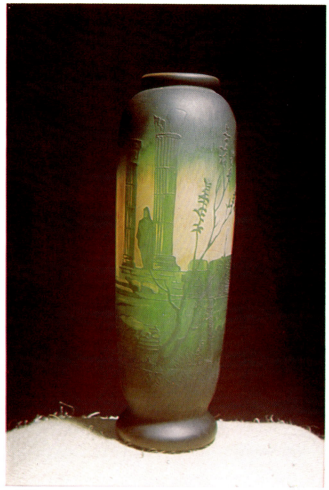

189.

Schneider. 10″ tall. There are two layers of glass with two acid cuttings. (Signature #125).

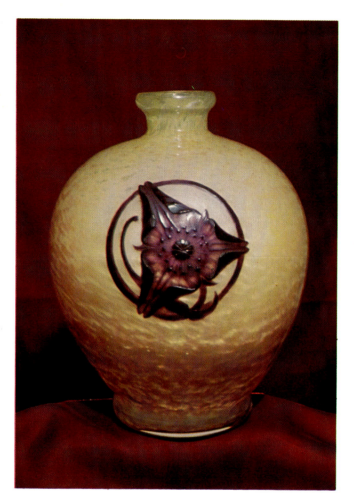

190.

Schneider. 11½″ tall. The dark glass in the center front of this vase was applied while the glass was still hot using a technique called "padding". This darker glass was then carved using wheel engraving to produce this stylized flower. The only cameo work in this piece is in the applied dark glass. (Signature #124).

191.

D. Christian Meisenthal. 6" tall. Three layers of glass. There was a single acid cutting and the blossoms and portions of the vine of the morning glory were then finished with wheel engraving. (Signature #131).

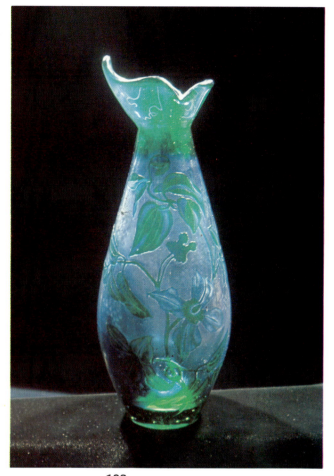

192.

D. Christian Meisenthal. 12" tall. The clematis floral decoration in layers of green and blue glass on clear was produced in large part by acid cutting but with some wheel engraving in the finishing process, particularly in the leaves and blossoms. The "hammered metal" appearance in several areas of the surface was produced by wheel cutting. (Signature #127).

193.

D. Christian Meisenthal. 6¼" tall. Four layers of glass. A single acid cutting was used and the floral design was then expertly cut using the engraving wheel.

194.

Val St. Lambert. 10" tall. Three acid cuttings were used to produce this harbor scene in this double layered glass vase. The white portion of the sea gull in the lower half of the vase is actually intaglio since the white body is produced by cutting into the blue surface, whereas the blue head of this bird is in cameo relief. (Signature #129).

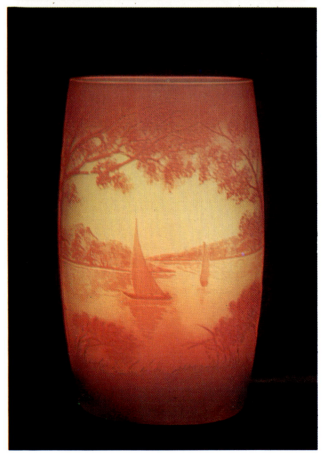

195.

Val St. Lambert. 9½" tall. This scenic vase was produced from a blank of two glass layers with three acid cuttings. (In the collection of Mr. and Mrs. Rex Cook).

196.

(A) Val St. Lambert bottle. 6½" tall. (Signature #126).

(B) Baccarat. 7½" tall. (Signature #133).

(C) St. Louis. 5½" tall. (Signature #132).

(D) Val St. Lambert. 6½" tall. (Signature #128).

(E) Unsigned. 11" tall.

197.

Val St. Lambert. Tumbler is 4" tall and pitcher is 14" tall. Both were formed from blanks of two layers of glass with acid cutting in the surface. The foliage has had some wheel engraving in the finishing process. Note the mottled background which has been produced by acid cutting. (Signature #123 was copied from base of tumbler).

198.

Verrerie d'Art de Lorraine; B, S & Company. (Burgun and Schverer).

(A) 5¾" tall. The color in the flowers is trapped between layers of glass, and the clear surface glass has been carved in cameo relief over the colored areas. In the finishing process a "hammered metal" effect has been produced in the surface of the glass in several areas.

(B) 3¼" tall. Technique in this piece is the same as "A" with the colored portions trapped between layers of glass and with the glass over the colored areas carved in cameo relief.

199.

Verrerie d'Art de Lorraine; B, S & Company (Burgun and Schverer). 6" tall. Most of the unwanted glass has been removed by acid cutting; however, the foliage has been carved with the engraving wheel. (Signature #134).

200.

(A) Croismare G. V. 9½″ tall. (Signature #135).

(B) Vallerysthal. 7½″ tall. The vine and raspberries have been wheel engraved. Note the fine acid cut pattern in the background. (Signature #136).

(C) Yean. 8½″ tall. (Signature #137).

(D) Roger. 9″ tall. (Signature #142).

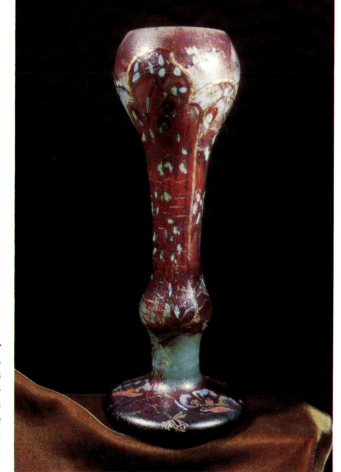

201.

Vallerysthal. 12″ tall. Close inspection reveals considerable detail in the work of the surface of this vase. Much of the detail is produced by acid cutting. Fine bits of foil are incorporated under the thin outside red layer. There is enamel and gold gilt decoration. Enamel signature.

202.

(A) Michel. 12″ tall. In this scenic vase there are four layers of glass with three acid cuttings. (Signature #145).

(B) Michel. 10″ tall. Only two acid cuttings in this three layered vase were required to produce this Venetian scene. Signature is same as in "A".

203.

(A) Arsall. 7½″ tall. Two acid cuttings in this double layer vase.

(B) Arsall. 8″ tall. Two acid cuttings, two glass layers. (Signature #146).

(C) Michel. 8½″ tall. This vase has three layers of glass with two acid cuttings.

204.

Deveay. 12½″ tall. There are three layers of glass with only two acid cuttings. (Signature #139).

205.

D'Aurys. 10″ tall. Four layers of glass with three acid cuttings. (Signature #138).

206.

Sèvres. 8″ tall. Dated 1900. This nasturtium design was produced in this vase with four glass layers with six acid cuttings. (Signature #144).

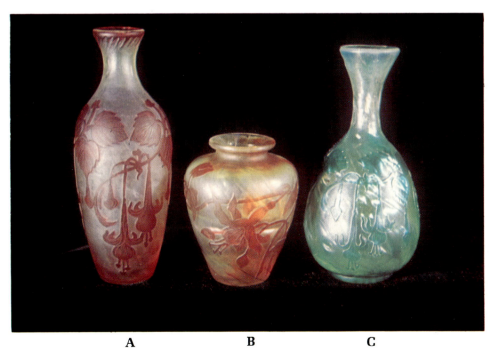

A B C

207.

Pantin. These three vases are all products of the Cristallerie de Pantin and each is signed differently. Note the iridescence in these pieces, more evident in "B" and "C".

(A) 6½″ tall. (Signature #153).

(B) 3¾″ tall. (Signature #156).

(C) 6″ tall. (In the collection of Mr. Ray Keller). (Signature #157).

208.

Harrach. 8″ tall. Four glass layers, three acid cuttings and a small amount of wheel engraving. (In the collection of Mr. Ray Keller). (Signature #148).

209.

Loetz. 11½″ tall. Three glass layers with two acid cuttings. (In the collection of Mr. and Mrs. William Arbeiter).

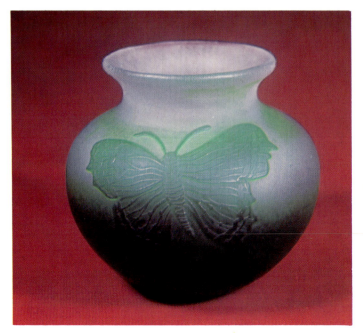

210.

Kosta. 2½″ tall. Made in Sweden in the French style. (In the collection of Mr. and Mrs. William Arbeiter). (Signature #147).

211.

(A) Bohemia. This covered box is 4" tall and signed in enamel on the base. On the pictoral surface of the bowl is the name "K. Schaffer". (Signature #150).

(B) D'Argental. 4" tall. Two glass layers, two acid cuttings. (Signature #120).

212.

Jacques Gruber. Plaque measures approximately 11½" by 5" in greatest dimensions. There are five acid cuttings in the surface of this plaque. Unfortunately there are some damaged areas in this piece. (Signature #151).

213.

These six vases are all miniatures. Note the presence of the gentleman's ring which was placed in this photograph for the purpose of emphasizing the relative sizes of these pieces.

(A) Michel. 3⅛" tall.

(B) Daum. 1½" tall.

(C) Daum. 1⅝" tall.

(D) Daum. 1⅝" tall.

(E) Daum. 1½" tall.

(F) Michel. 3¼" tall.

(A, B, C, D and E are in the collection of Mr. Ray Keller).

214.

(A) Legras. 11¼" tall. Four layers of glass with four acid cuttings.

(B) deVez. 7" tall. Three glass layers with two acid cuttings.

(C) Delatte. 11¼" tall. Three layers of glass with three acid cuttings.

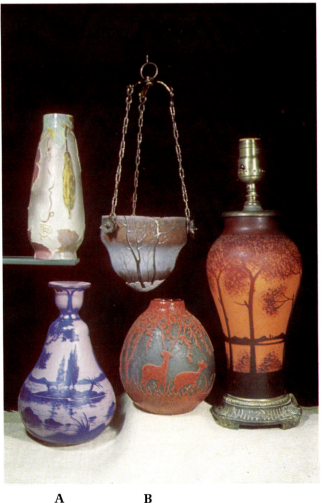

215.

(A) Perrier. See signature #152. 7½" tall. The vine, blossoms, and fruit of the summer squash is produced in this three layer glass vase with a single deep cutting and some line cutting within the foliage.

(B) Legras. Glass bowl is 4" tall. This hanging planter has an acid cut surface with enamel decoration on the trees and for the snow.

(C) deVez. 8" tall. Three layers of glass with two acid cuttings.

(D) Legras. 6" tall. A single acid cutting was used in this vase of two layers of glass.

(E) Beauté. The glass portion is 10" tall. This piece was made to be a lamp and is not a vase converted to a lamp. The base is stamped "Czechoslovakia". (Signature #154).

216.

(A) Legras. 18″ tall. There are four layers of glass with four acid cuttings.

(B) Delatte. 14½″ tall. Two glass layers and two acid cuttings.

(C) Delatte. 6¾″ tall. Sweet pea design produced with two acid cuttings.

(D) Arsall. 10″ tall. Two acid cuttings in this three layer glass vase.

(E) Pantin. 17½″ tall. Three glass layers with two acid cuttings. (Signature #158).

217.

(A) Moser Karlsbad. 12″ tall. Two layers of glass with two acid cuttings. (Signature #159).

(B) V.S.L. (Val St. Lambert). 12″ tall. Two layers of glass with two acid cuttings. (Signature #130).

(C) Duguersil. 12″ tall. Surface is acid cut. All the brown color in the thistle is enameling. (Signature #160).

218.

(A) Baccarat. 6″ tall. Dated 1915. On back has the quotation "Qui sy Frotte sy Pique". Acid cut with some wheel engraving in the thistle pattern. (Signature #161).

(B) F.H. 6″ tall. Three layers of glass with a single acid cutting. (Signature #163).

(C) Nancea. 5½″ tall. Three glass layers. Single acid cutting and some enameling. (Signature #162).

(D) Silesia. 7″ tall. Three layers of glass. Two acid cuttings. (Signature #164).

219.

(A) Loetz. 10″ tall. (Signature #165).

(B) Degue. 5½″ tall. (Signature #171).

(C) P. Nicolas. 4¼″ tall. (Signature #169).

(D) G. Raspiller. 5¼″ tall. (Signature #167).

(E) Art. 10″ tall. (Signature #170).

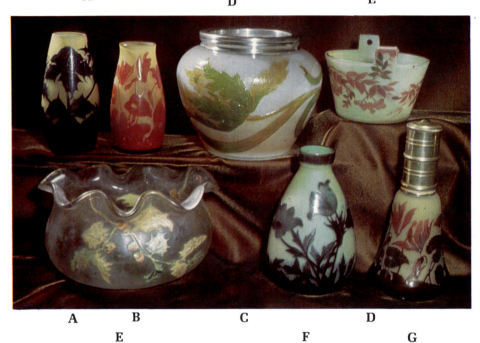

220.

(A) D'Argental. 5″ tall. Thistle pattern. (Signature #118).

(B) D'Argental. 4½″ tall.

(C) V.S. (signed on bottom), Lorraine (signed on side). 5½″ tall. (Signature #168).

(D) deVez. 3½″ tall. Variety of wild cherry in cameo outline in this bowl.

(E) J. Mabut. 4″ tall. Clear glass, acid cut with gold gilt and painting to color the holly decoration. Store name and address placed on bottom. (Signature #172).

(F) Delatte. 6″ tall. (Signature #112).

(G) D'Argental. 7″ tall. Scent bottle with wick and metal cover.

221.

(A) D'Aurys. 12″ tall. This wild thicket vine was produced by two acid cuttings from a blank consisting of three layers of glass. (Signature #141).

(B) L. Cie (St. Denis-Paris). 4″ tall. This three handled bowl has acid cut work in the surface with gold decoration.

(C) L. Cie. (St. Denis-Paris). 5″ tall. (Signature #175).

(D) Indiana, L. Cie. 12″ tall. The poppy is outlined in cameo relief. There is gold decoration at the top and base. The remaining outside surface is irregular and covered with brownish, semi-iridescent material. (Signature #176).

222.

(A) St. Ouen. 13½" tall. Three layers of glass with two acid cuttings. (Signature #189).

(B) Unsigned. 7" tall. Metallic flecks are present in the amber glass. Acid cutting with some wheel cutting of background.

(C) D'Argyl. 9" tall. Three glass layers with two acid cuttings.

(D) Val. 7½" tall. Frosted glass, acid cut and painted. (Signature #177).

223.

These five pieces are all produced by acid cutting in the surface of clear glass followed by decoration with enameling, painting, and gilt.

(A) Mont Joye. 4¼" tall. Acid cut work in the surface with an enameled poppy and gilt decoration.

(B) Pantin (T.S.V. and Co.). 5½" tall. (Signature #155).

(C) H. T. 5½" tall.

(D) Delatte. 5½" tall.

(E) Unsigned. 5" tall. Note detailed pattern in background similar to that produced in many Baccarat, Val St. Lambert, and St. Louis pieces.

224.

A   B   C   D   E   F

(A) Mont Joye. 12" tall. Clear glass, acid cut and frosted with gilt and enameled decoration. (Signature #178).

(B) Unsigned. 3" tall. Much wheel engraving as well as some intaglio decoration.

(C) Unsigned. 4½" tall. Much wheel engraving, mostly producing cameo decoration but with some intaglio.

(D) Graf Harrach. 6¼" tall. Acid cutting and wheel engraving in this two layer cameo piece. (Signature #149).

(E) Damon. 10" tall. Pale green glass on clear glass with acid cut work (Signature #179).

(F) Unsigned. 8½"

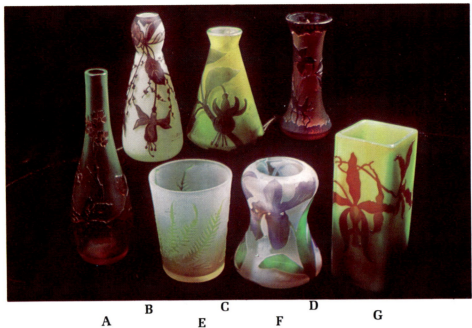

225.

(A) Heckert. 8″ tall. (Signature #174).

(B) Ciriama. 6″ tall. (Signature #185).

(C) Luscher. 5½″ tall. (Signature #182).

(D) LuB. 5″ tall. (Signature #183).

(E) Wanda. Tumbler is 4″ tall. (Signature #180).

(F) Aerozon D.R.G.M. 4½″ tall. Four layers of glass with two acid cuttings. (Signature #181).

(G) Unsigned. 6″ tall.

226.

(A) Chouvenin. 10″ tall. Acid cut and painted. (Signature #186).

(B) Weis. 4″ tall. Three layers of glass with a single acid cutting. (Signature #190).

(C) Chouvenin. 5½″ tall. Acid cut and painted. (Signature #187).

(D) Bar. 6½″ tall. Two layers of glass with two acid cuttings. (Signature #184).

227.

(A) Lorraine. 4½″ tall. 9″ diameter. Clear glass. Acid cut with enameling of the relief outlined areas. Silver plated metal rim about the top edge. (Signature #188).

(B) Moda. Bowl is 7½″ in diameter and 4″ tall. Clear glass. Acid cut and painted. (Signature #191).

(C) Unsigned but numbered. diameter. 2″ tall. Dark red glass green was subjected to acid cutting and then gold decoration produce this raspberry design.

(D) Legras. 8″ diameter. 2¼″ ta Clear green glass which is a cut in the bowl portion.

228.

All four of these pieces are unsigned.

(A) 15½″ tall.

(B) 16″ tall.

(C) 16″ tall.

(D) 19″ tall. (Note similarity to Le Verre Francais).

229.

(A) Arsall. 11½″ tall. Three layers of glass with three acid cuttings. (Signature #143).

(B) Legras. 8″ tall. Dark green glass was acid cut and decorated. Etched on the base is the following: "Made in France exclusively for Paris decorators". — Strange that glass made in a suburb of Paris should have an inscription in English if made for market in France.

(C) Unsigned. 8½″ tall. Acid cut and decorated. An obviously fake "E. Galle" signature has been cut into the base.

(D) Croismare G. V. 13½″ tall. Two layers of glass with two acid cuttings.

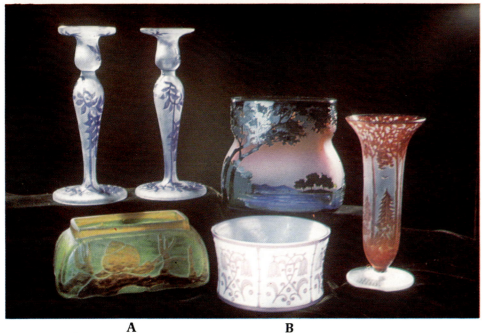

230.

All of these are unsigned.

(A) Each of these candlesticks is 9″ tall. Two layers of glass with two acid cuttings.

(B) 6″ tall. Five acid cuttings were used in this vase of three layers of glass.

(C) 4″ tall. Note similarity to Le Verre Francais.

(D) This bowl is 6″ in diameter and 3½″ tall. Two acid cuttings were used in the surface of this bowl which consists of three layers of glass.

(E) 8″ tall. Two layers of glass with two acid cuttings.

Lamps

231.

Daum. 18¾" tall. The base and shade are both decorated with a grape design with an unusual background. There are applied bits of glass to both the shade and vase in the form of cabochons forming grapes. There are two glass snails applied to the base of this lamp.

232.

(A) Daum. 19" tall. Acid cut and decorated.

(B) Daum. 19½" tall. Cockscomb in cameo relief.

(C) Daum. 18" tall. Cameo work in both shade and base is acid cut.

233.

Daum. 29¼″ tall. This lamp weighs 18 lbs. There are two layers of glass with two acid cuttings both in the shade and in the base of the lamp. (Signature #84).

234.

Daum. 14″ tall. This rain scene is acid cut and decorated.

235.

(A) Daum. 14″ tall, acid cut and decorated.

(B) This scenic vase is 13½″ tall. There is deep acid cutting both in the base and in the shade.

131

236

(A) Gallé. 14″ tall. There are nine butterflies in cameo relief in the shade of this vase.

(B) Gallé. 23″ tall. Gallé signature on the base is without star, but with a star on the shade.

(C) Gallé. 14″ tall. Two eagles are present in cameo relief on the shade above the scenic base.

237.

(A) Gallé. 12½″ tall. The caramel-colored glass has been cut away behind the blossoms so that the blue blossoms show to better advantage. when the lamp is lighted.

(B) Gallé. 14″ tall. Clematis design.

238.

(A) Gallé. 11″ tall. Shade and base have four layers of glass with four acid cuttings. Glass has been cut away from the inside surface of the shade and base behind the blossoms so that these areas show brighter when the lamp is lighted.

(B) Gallé. 10½″ tall. Six rooks in flight are carved in the shade.

239.

Gallé. 12½″ tall. Note the floral design in the shade and base stands out as a result of being mold blown as well as due to cameo relief. (In the collection of Mr. and Mrs. William Arbeiter).

240.

(A) Le Verre Francais. 14½″ tall.

(B) Geef Lyon. 18″ tall. There are four acid cut cameo panels in this shade, each representing one of the four seasons. The base is porcelain. Mountings are metal with four crystals decorating the shade. (Signature #192).

241.

Gallé corner light. This light fixture is 10″ in vertical height. This rare type light fixture has a glass shade in front enclosed with a metal frame with the flower design in the metal matching that in the glass. (Signature #28).

242.

These three lamps are all night lights.

(A) Daum. 6½″ tall. Three layer cameo with three acid cuttings.

(B) Muller. 9½″ tall. Three layers of glass with three acid cuttings.

(C) Le Verre Francais. 7″ tall. Two layers of glass with a single acid cutting.

243.

Gallé bowl-type chandelier. 17½" in diameter. Deeply cut with three acid cuttings with some wheel engraving of portions of the cut surface.

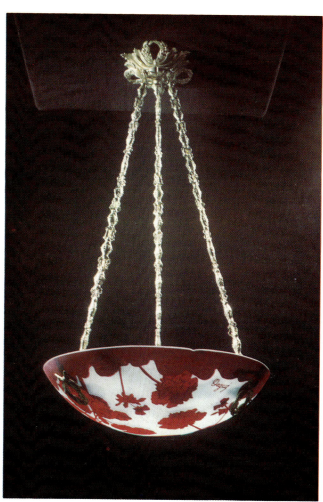

244.

Degue. Bowl-type chandelier. 13½" diameter. Two layers of glass and two acid cuttings producing a geranium decoration. (Signature #166).

245.

Gallé ball-type chandelier. The glass ball is 10½" in vertical height.

246.

Chinese or Peking cameo. Carving is all accomplished without the aid of acid cutting.

(A) 7½″ tall. (In the collection of Mr. and Mrs. William Arbeiter).

(B) 3¾″ tall. (In the collection of Mr. and Mrs. William Arbeiter).

247.

Chinese or Peking cameo.

(A) 10″ tall. Two birds appear in cameo relief on the back side of this vase.

(B) Bowl is 3¼″ tall and 9¾″ in diameter.

(C) 4¾″ tall. Oriental signature on bottom. There are three layers of glass, all of which are very similar in color, and which are readily evident only by examination of the top edge.

(D) Bottle is 5″ tall.

(E) Covered box is 5½″ tall. Single color of glass.

248.
English cameo.

(A) Webb. 9″ tall. Signed "Thomas Webb & Sons. Cameo". Foliage carved with wheel engraving. (In the collection of Mr. and Mrs. William Arbeiter).

(B) Spirit flask or scent bottle. 10¼″ long. Signed "patent". Hall-marked silver top. Three different types of flowers are expertly carved in three layer cameo on one side of this cut crystal bottle.

249.
English cameo.

(A) Stevens and Williams. 4″ tall. Butterfly carved into surface of back side of this vase. (In the collection of Mr. and Mrs. William Arbeiter).

(B) Webb. 6″ tall and 9″ in diameter. Most of the glass cutting was accomplished with acid with some wheel cutting of the blossoms.

(C) Shade for fairy lamp. 4″ tall. Unsigned, but presumably Stevens and Williams, as cameo design, including butterfly, is almost identical to that in "A" above, except that the ginko branches are directed downward in the vase and upward in the shade.

(D) Stevens and Williams. 6″ tall. All cutting in surface was accomplished with wheel engraving. Note the Oriental style. There is clear glass between the opaque white and black layers which is not present in the Chinese pieces illustrated.

250.

Tiffany cameo. 12″ tall. Good carving is evident in the surface of this vase. (In the collection of Mr. and Mrs. William Arbeiter).

251.

Steuben acid cut-back. 12″ tall. (In the collection of Mr. and Mrs. William Arbeiter).

252.

Steuben acid cut-back. 10″ tall. (In the collection of Mr. and Mrs. William Arbeiter).

All signatures from cameo glass reproduced in actual size.

1. Cameo (Photo 8)
2. Cameo ("F" in photo 81)
3. Cameo ("D" in photo 86)
4. Cameo ("A" in photo 74)
5. Cameo ("A" in photo 67)
6. Cameo (photo 58)
7. Cameo ("F" in photo 86)
8. Cameo ("B" in photo 74)
9. Cameo ("D" in photo 50)
10. Cameo ("B" in photo 78)
11. Engraved (photo 59)
12. Engraved ("A" in photo 35)
13. Cameo ("A" in photo 80)
14. Cameo ("E" in photo 82)
15. Cameo ("B" in photo 16)
16. Cameo ("B" in photo 44)
17. Engraved (photo 4)

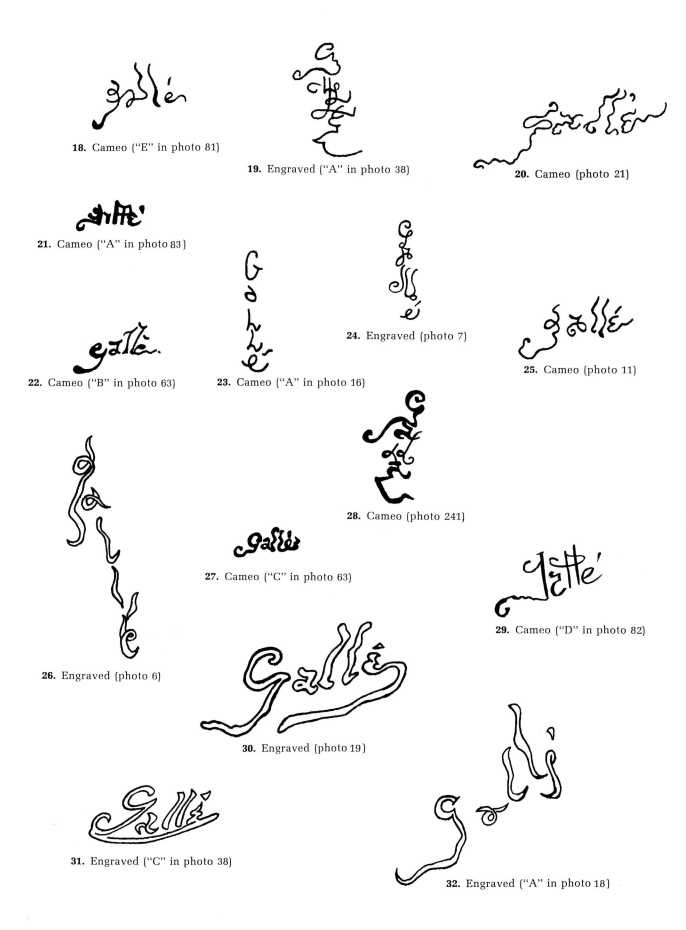

18. Cameo ("E" in photo 81)

19. Engraved ("A" in photo 38)

20. Cameo (photo 21)

21. Cameo ("A" in photo 83)

22. Cameo ("B" in photo 63)

23. Cameo ("A" in photo 16)

24. Engraved (photo 7)

25. Cameo (photo 11)

26. Engraved (photo 6)

27. Cameo ("C" in photo 63)

28. Cameo (photo 241)

29. Cameo ("D" in photo 82)

30. Engraved (photo 19)

31. Engraved ("C" in photo 38)

32. Engraved ("A" in photo 18)

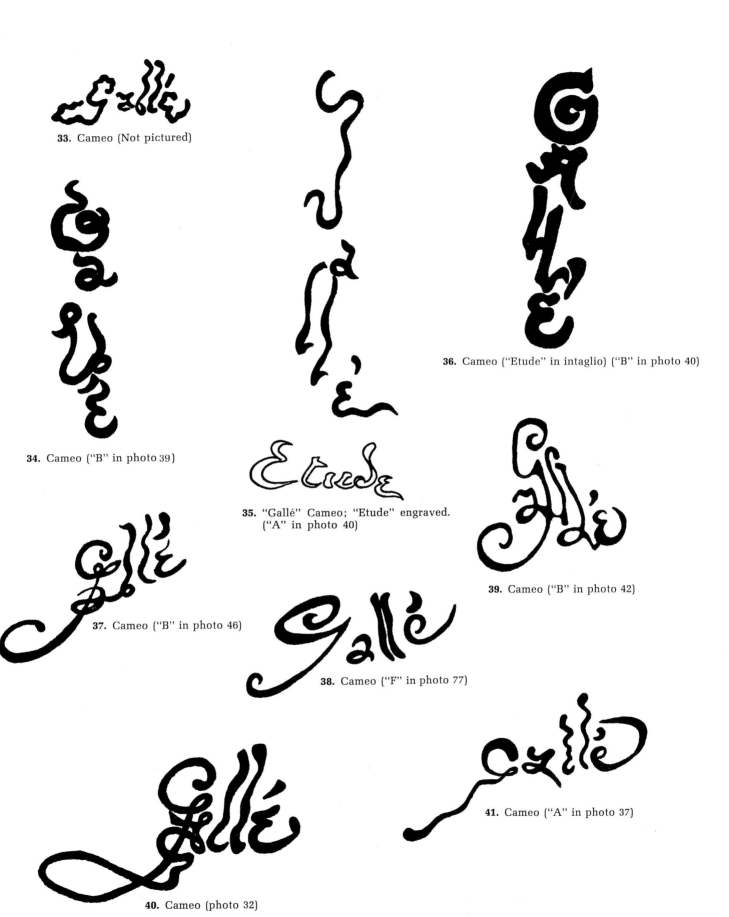

42. Cameo ("B" in photo 37)

43. Cameo (photo 23)

44. Cameo (photo 14)

45. Cameo ("A" in photo 45)

46. Cameo (photo 41)

47. Cameo ("B" in photo 43)

48. Cameo (photo 5)

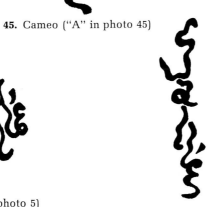

49. Cameo ("C" in photo 76)

50. Cameo ("B" in photo 1)

51. Cameo ("B" in photo 35)

52. Cameo ("C" in photo 37)

53. Cameo. "E‡G" engraved. (photo 13).

54. Engraved (photo 65)

55. Cameo (photo 12)

56. Acid-cut intaglio (photo 71)

57. Cameo ("D" in photo 81)

58. Engraved (photo 9)

59. Engraved ("B" in photo 18)

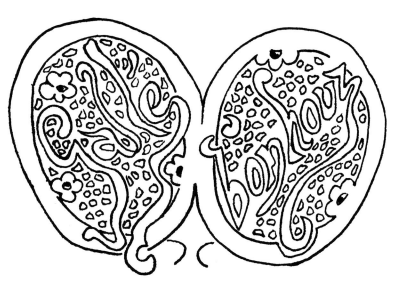

60. Cameo ("A" in photo 42)

61. Cameo ("A" in photo 50)

62. Cameo (photo 54)

63. Cameo ("A" in photo 44)

64. Cameo ("B" in photo 84)

65. Cameo "Modele et Decor Deposes" scratched in margin of base. (photo 10)

66. Engraved ("B" in photo 17)

67. Engraved (photo 20)

69. Engraved ("A" in photo 17)

68. Engraved (not pictured)

71. Etched (photo 91)

70. Engraved and gold gilt (photo 92)

72. Gold gilt ("D" in photo 132)

73. Engraved and gold gilt ("B" in photo 100)

74. Engraved ("A" in photo 100)

76. Cameo (photo 110)

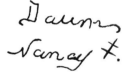

75. Cameo ("B" in photo 137)

77. Enamel (photo 109)

78. Engraved (photo 87)

80. Enamel ("B" in photo 113)

81. Cameo ("C" in photo 121)

79. Engraved ("B" in photo 89)

82. Engraved (photo 94)

83. Engraved (photo 116)

Shade

Base

84. Cameo (photo 233)

85. Cameo ("A" in photo 111)

86. Enamel ("G" in photo 113)

87. Engraved and gold gilt ("D" in photo 142)

88. Engraved and gold gilt ("B" in photo 93)

89. Enamel (photo 103)

90. Engraved and gold gilt ("A" in photo 93)

91. Engraved and gold gilt (photo 97)

92. Engraved ("B" in photo 114)

93. Engraved and gold gilt (photo 88)

94. Engraved (photo 102)

95. Cameo (photo 156)

96. Engraved ("C" in photo 154)

97. Enamel (photo 145)

98. Engraved (photo 151)

99. Cameo ("B" in photo 148)

100. Cameo (photo 147)

101. Signature in intaglio; moth in cameo. (photo 153)

102. Engraved ("B" in photo 154)

103. Cameo (photo 146)

104. Cameo (photo 160)

105. Cameo (photo 161)

106. Cameo (not pictured)

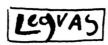
107. Cameo ("A" in photo 167)

108. Cameo (photo 170)

109. Cameo (photo 176)

110. Cameo ("C" in photo 173)

111. Cameo ("A" in photo 172)

114. Cameo ("B" in photo 172)

112. Cameo ("F" in photo 220)

113. Engraved ("B" in photo 180)

115. Etched. Also "candy cane" marker ("B" in photo 182)

117. Engraved ("C" in photo 180)

116. Engraved. "Charder" in cameo. ("A" in photo 180)

118. Cameo ("A" in photo 220)

119. Cameo (photo 185)

120. Engraved ("B" in photo 211)

121. Cameo ("D" in photo 183)

122. Cameo ("E" in photo 183)

123. Engraved ("A" in photo 197)

124. Etched (photo 190)

125. Engraved (photo 189)

126. Engraved ("A" in photo 196)

127. Cameo (photo 192)

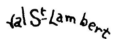

128. Engraved ("D" in photo 196)

129. Cameo (photo 194)

130. Cameo ("B" in photo 217)

131. Engraved (photo 191)

132. Etched ("C" in photo 196)

BACCARAT

133. Etched ("B" in photo 196)

134. Gold gilt (photo 199)

135. Cameo ("A" in photo 200)

136. Engraved ("B" in photo 200)

139. Cameo (photo 204)

137. Cameo ("C" in photo 200)

138. Cameo (photo 205)

142. Cameo ("D" in photo 200)

140. Cameo ("A" in photo 213)

141. Cameo ("A" in photo 221)

145. Cameo ("A" in photo 202)

143. Cameo ("A" in photo 229)

144. Engraved and gold gilt (photo 206)

147. Engraved (photo 210)

146. Cameo ("B" in photo 203)

148. Cameo (photo 208)

149. Engraved ("D" in photo 224)

150. Enamel ("A" in photo 211)

151. Engraved (photo 212)

152. Cameo ("A" in photo 215)

153. Engraved ("A" in photo 207)

154. Engraved ("E" in photo 215)

155. Gold gilt ("B" in photo 223)

156. Engraved ("B" in photo 207)

157. Engraved ("C" in photo 207)

158. Engraved ("E" in photo 216)

159. Cameo ("A" in photo 217)

160. Enamel ("C" in photo 217)

161. Engraved ("A" in photo 218)

F.H.

162. Enamel ("C" in photo 218) 163. Cameo ("B" in photo 218)

Silesia

164. Engraved ("D" in photo 218)

165. Cameo ("A" in photo 219)

166. Cameo (photo 244)

167. Cameo ("D" in photo 219)

P. Nicolas

Cut

170. Cameo ("E" in photo 219)

169. Engraved ("C" in photo 219)

168. Etched. "Lorraine" on side is in cameo. ("C" in photo 220)
(Portions of ship may not be accurate as this area of signature was indistinct)

171. Cameo ("B" in photo 219)

172. Gold gilt ("E" in photo 220)

D'ARGYL

173. Cameo ("C" in photo 222)

Heckert.

174. Cameo ("A" in photo 225)

175. Gold gilt ("C" in photo 221)

176. Gold gilt ("D" in photo 221)

177. Enamel ("D" in photo 222)

178. Gold gilt ("A" in photo 224)

179. Engraved ("E" in photo 224)

180. Cameo. Could be made for "Wanda" rather than by "Wanda" ("E" in photo 225)

181. Cameo ("F" in photo 225)

182. Cameo ("C" in photo 225)

183. Engraved ("D" in photo 225)

184. Engraved ("D" in photo 226)

185. Cameo ("B" in photo 225)

186. Enamel ("A" in photo 226)

187. Enamel ("C" in photo 226)

188. Enamel ("A" in photo 227)

189. Engraved ("A" in photo 222)

190. Cameo ("B" in photo 226)

191. Cameo ("B" in photo 227)

192. Cameo ("B" in photo 240)

153

Glass Through the Ages. E. Barrington Hayes. Penguin Books Inc. Baltimore, Maryland. 1966.

Glass and Crystal, Volume I. Elka Schrijver. Universe Books Inc. New York, New York. 1964.

Glass and Crystal, Volume II. Elka Schrijver. Universe Books Inc. New York, New York. 1964.

Modern Glass. Guiloaume Janneau. The Studios Ltd. 1931.

Modern Glass. Ada Polak. Faber and Faber. London. 1962.

Nineteenth Century Cameo Glass. Geoffrey W. Beard. The Ceramic Book Company. Newport, Monmouthshire, England. 1956.

English Nineteenth Century Cameo Glass. The Corning Museum of Glass. Corning, New York. 1963.

Nineteenth Century Glass, Its Genesis and Development. Albert Christian Revi. Thomas Nelson and Sons. New York, New York. 1967.

Art Glass Nouveau. Ray and Lee Grover. Charles E. Tuttle. Rutland, Vermont. 1967.

The Flowering of Art Nouveau. Maurice Rheims. Harry N. Abrams, Inc. New York. **1963**.

L'Objet 1900. Maurice Rheims. Arts et Metiers Graphiques. Paris. 1964.

French Cameo Glass. Albert Christian Revi. Spinning Wheel. **14:** 24-26 and 43, March, 1958.

Le cas étrange de Monsieur Gallé (Les Verres de Gallé). Hélène Demoriane. Connaissance des arts. **102:** 34-41, 1960.

The Glass of Emile Gallé. Richard Dennis. Antiques International. 182-192, 1966. Michael Joseph Ltd. London.

Three Art Nouveau Glass Makers. William B. O'Neal. Journal of Glass Studies. **2:** 125-138, 1960.

Signatures on Gallé Glass. Ada Polak. Journal of Glass Studies. **8:** 120-123, 1966.

Gallé Glass: Luxurious, Cheap and Imitated. Ada Polak. Journal of Glass Studies. **5:** 105-115, 1963.

Daum et la Cristallerie Francaise. P.-M. Grand. Editions Tallandier. Fevrier 1963.

Les Verreries de Daum. L'Illustration Economique et Financiere (Numero de Meurthe-et-Moselle). 1925.

Michel Daum. Personal Communications.

Schneider Art Glass. John W. Graves. Spinning Wheel. **23:** 10-11 and 43, October 1967.

John W. Graves. Personal Communications.

The "Fourth" Paperweight Factory. Albert Christian Revi. Spinning Wheel. **22:** 10-11 and 45, October 1966.

Emile Gallé. L. de Fourcaud. Revue de L'Art. **11:** 34-44, 1902.

Emile Gallé. L. de Fourcaud. Revue de L'Art. **11:** 171-186, 1902.

Emile Gallé. L. de Fourcaud. Revue de L'Art. **12:** 337-353, 1902.

Emile Gallé, Psychologie de l'artist et synthese de l'oeuvre. Roger Marx. Art et Decoration. **15:** 233-252, Aout 1911.

Emile Gallé—A Master in Glass. Prince B. Karageorgevitch. The Magazine of Art. **2:** 310-314, 1904.

The Glass Makers of Nancy France. Thelma Shull. Hobbies. **47:** 56-57, September 1942.

Annuaire des Ceramistes et Verriers de France et des Industries s'y Rattachant. 1935 Edition.

acid cut-back, 11

Aerozon D. R. Y. M., **128, 153**

Argy-Rousseau, G., 15

Arsall, 24, **120, 125, 129, 150**

Art, **126, 152**

B S & Co., 24

Baccarat, 24, **117, 125, 149, 151**

Barberini vase, 10

Bar, **128, 153**

Beaute, **124, 151**

Boberg, Ferdinand, 25

Bohemia, **123, 151**

Bowman, A. E., 25

Brocard, Joseph, 18, 20

Burgun and Schverer, 7, 24, **118, 150**

cabochon, 14, 18, **17(B), 108, 123**

cameo glass, definition, 9

cameo glass, production of, 11, 12, 13

"candy cane", 23, **182(B)**

Charder, 23, **180(A), 148**

Carder, Frederick, 10, 11

Chinese (Peking) Cameo, 9, 10, **136**

Chouvenin, **128, 153**

Christian, D. (Meisenthal) 24, **115, 149**

Ciriama, **128, 153**

"Clair de Lune", 18

Cristallerie de La Villette, 22

Cristallerie de Nancy, 21

Cristallerie de Pantin, 22, **121, 125, 151**

Croismare (see Muller)

Croismare G. V., **119, 129, 150**

Cros, Henri, 15

D'Argental, 7, 24, **112, 113, 122, 126, 148**

D'Argyl, **127, 152**

Dammouse, Albert, 15

Damon, **127, 153**

Daum, 7, 15, 19, 20, 21, 23, 25, **66-91, 123, 130, 131, 134, 145, 146**

Daum, Antonin, 20, 21

Daum, Auguste, 20, 21

Daum, Henri, 21

Daum, Jacques, 21

Daum, Jean, 20

Daum, Michel, 7, 21

Daum, Paul, 21

D'Aurys, **121, 126, 150**

Décorchemont, Francois, 15

Degue, **126, 135, 152**

Delatte, A., 23, **108, 109, 124-127, 148**

Despret, George, 15

de Varreux, M., 22

DeVeay, **120, 150**

deVez, 22, **106, 107, 124, 126, 148**

Duguensil, **125, 151**

Ecole de Nancy (School of Nancy), 19, 21, 25

English cameo, 9, 10, **137**

F. H., **125, 152**

G R (Gallé-Reinemer), 17

Gallé, Charles, 17

Gallé, Emile, 15-21, 25, **28-65, 132-135, 139-144**

Gruber, Jacques, 26, **123, 151**

Hadelands, 11, 25

Harrach, **122, 127, 151**

Heckert, **128, 152**

Hesteaux, 19

Hodgett, Joshua, 10

hydrofloric acid, 9, 10, 12

intaglio, 9, 14, **96, 98, 100, 101, 127**

Kosta, 11, 25, **122, 150**

L. & Cie, **126, 152**

Lang, Emile, 19

Legras, August J. F., 22, **104, 105, 124, 125, 128, 129, 148**

Léveillé, 16

Le Verre Francais, 23, **110, 134, 148**

Loetz, 11, 26, **122, 126, 152**

Lorraine, **128, 153**

Lorraine, cross of, 15

Lu B, **128, 153**

Luscher, **128, 153**

Lyon, Geef, **134, 153**

Mabut, J., **126, 152**

Majorelle, 19

Marinot, Maurice, 25

marquetry, "marquetrie de verre" 14, **33**

Meisenthal (D. Christian), 24, **115, 149**

Michel, 26, **120, 123, 150**

Michel, Edward, 26

Moda, **128, 153**

Monot; Monot and Stumpf; etc., 22

Mont Joye, 22, **127, 153**

Moser, 26, **125, 151**

Muller (Croismare, Luneville, Nancy), 21, **92-101, 134, 147**

Nancea, **125, 152**

Nicolas, Paul, 26, **126, 152**

Northwood, John, 10

padding, 14, 18, **73, 89, 90, 114**

Pantin, 22, **121, 125, 127, 151**

pâte de verre, 14, 15

"paysages de verre", 18

Pegasus vase, 10

Peking (Chinese) Cameo, 9, 10, **136**

Pfohl, Karl, 10

Portland Vase, 10

Prouvé, Victor, 19

Raspiller, G., **126, 152**

Reijmyre, 11, 25

Richard, 24, **111, 149**

Roger, **119, 150**

Rousseau, Eugène, 15, 16, 18, 20

Saint Hiliare, Touvier, de Varreux & Company, 22

Saint Louis, 24, **117, 149**

St. Ouen, **127, 153**

Schneider, 7, 25, **114, 149**

Schaffer, K., **123, 151**

School of Nancy (Ecole de Nancy), 19, 21, 25

Selicia, **125, 152**

Sèvres, **207, 150**

signatures: discussion, 15, 16; illustrations, **139-153**

Steuben, 11, **138**

Stumpf, Touvier, Violette & Company, 22

Tiffany, **138**

Val, **127, 152**

Vallerysthal, 24, **119, 150**

Val Saint Lambert, 24, **116, 117, 125, 149**

Verrerie d'Art de Lorraine, 24

Verrerie de Nancy, 20

"verrière paralante", 18

Walter, Almeric, 15

Wanda, **128, 153**

Weis, **128, 153**

Wenneberg, Gunnar Gunnarson, 25

Woodall, George, 10

Woodall, Thomas, 10

Yean, **119, 150**

Zach, F., 10